CCNP Enterprise Advanced Routing and Services (ENARSI 300-410) Exam Practice Questions & Dumps

Exam Study Guide for CCNP Enterprise Advanced Routing and Services
(ENARSI 300-410) Latest Version

Presented By: Books Fortune

Copyright © 2020 by Books fortune

All rights reserved, including the rights to recreate this book or portions thereof in any manner whatsoever without the written confirmation of the publisher with the exception of the use of quotations in a book review and a few other noncommercial uses acceptable by copyright law.

First Copy Printed in 2020

About Books Fortune:

Books fortune is a publishing house based in Dallas, Texas, USA. It is a platform that is open both online & offline. It has played a key part in providing textbooks and other curriculum materials including literary collection, poetry & many other book genres. Books Fortune was founded in 2015, and is now distributing books worldwide.

Note: Find answers of the questions at the end of the book.

QUESTION 1

Automatic 6-to-4 tunnels take place among dual-stack routers (A, B, and C). One router has the IPv6 address, 2002:D030:6BC0:173C::26:37D0/48

Which of the given addresses is the IPv4 address of the router with the IPv6 address 2002:D030:6BC0:173C::26:37D0/48?

A. 10.176.15.131
B. 10.200.80.67
C. 208.48.107.192
D. 208.138.16.110

QUESTION 2

You have in recent times joined a corporation as the network administrator. You have been asked to complete the configuration on the border routers for an automatic 6-to-4 tunnel among several IPv6 network domains. The commands that are presently configured on the routers are as follows:

ipv6 route tunnel interface tunnel ipv6 address tunnel source

Which of the given additional commands are crucial to complete the configuration of automatic 6-to-4 tunnel on the border routers?

A. tunnel mode ipv6ip
B. tunnel mode ipv6ip 6to4
C. tunnel mode ipv6ip auto-tunnel
D. tunnel mode ipv6ip isatap

QUESTION 3

You have performed IPv6 automatic 6-to-4 tunneling among three IPv6 subnets as presented in the network display. (Click the Display(s) button.)

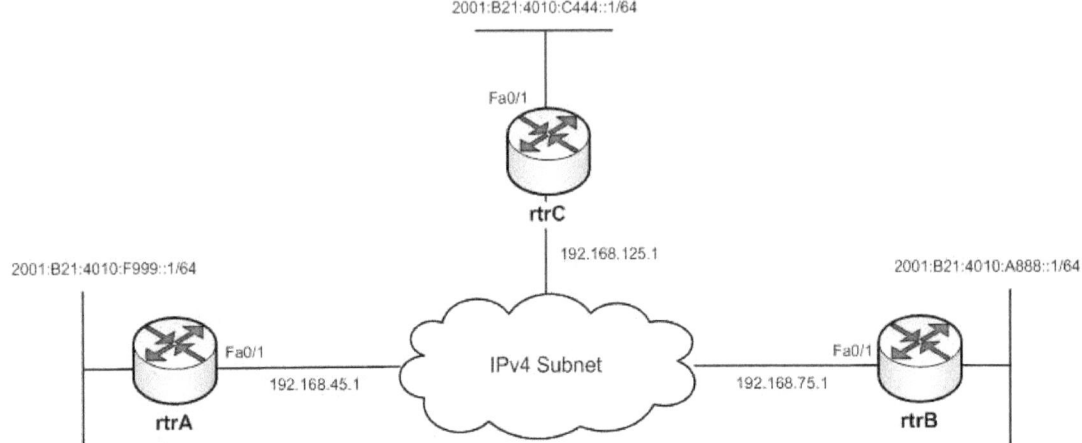

You have used the given commands to execute the automatic 6-to-4 tunnel:

```
rtrA(config)# interface Fa0/1
rtrA(config-if)# ip address 192.168.45.1 255.255.255.0
rtrA(config-if)# exit
rtrA(config)# interface Tunnel0
rtrA(config-if)# no ip address
rtrA(config-if)# tunnel mode ipv6ip 6to4
rtrA(config-if)# tunnel source Fa0/1
rtrA(config-if)# ipv6 address 2002:c0a8:2d01::1/64

rtrB(config)# interface Fa0/1
rtrB(config-if)# ip address 192.168.75.1 255.255.255.0
rtrB(config-if)# exit
rtrB(config)# interface Tunnel0
rtrB(config-if)# no ip address
rtrBconfig-if)# tunnel mode ipv6ip 6to4
rtrBconfig-if)# tunnel source Fa0/1
rtrBconfig-if)# ipv6 address 2002:c0a8:7d01::1/64

rtrC(config)# interface Fa0/1
rtrC(config-if)# ip address 192.168.125.1 255.255.255.0
rtrC(config-if)# exit
rtrC(config)# interface Tunnel0
rtrC(config-if)# no ip address
rtrC(config-if)# tunnel mode ipv6ip 6to4
rtrC(config-if)# tunnel source Fa0/1
rtrC(config-if)# ipv6 address 2002:c0a8:4b01::1/64
```

Your supervisor has appointed the task of verifying the automatic 6-to-4 tunnel to one of your colleagues. Your colleague runs the show running-config command and finds that incorrect IPv6 addresses have been appointed to the tunnel interfaces of the routers.

Which of the given IPv6 addresses must be appointed to rectify the issue? (Select two.)

A. 2002::c0a8:2d01/64 to the Fa0/1 interface of rtrA
B. 2002:c0a8:4b01::1/64 to the Fa0/1 interface of rtrB
C. 2002:c0a8:7d01::1/64 to the Fa0/1 interface of rtrC
D. 2002:c0a8:4b01::1/64 to the Fa0/1 interface of rtrA

QUESTION 4

An automatic IPv4-compatible IPv6 tunnel take places among two IPv6 networks. The two IPv6 networks belong to different BGP autonomous systems (AS). The tunnel source has the IPv4 address 172.168.111.65/24 and the tunnel destination has the IPv4 address 172.168.222.80/24.

Which of the given statements is ACCURATE about the tunnel source and tunnel destination IPv6 addresses? (Select two.)

A. the IPv6 address of the tunnel source is 172.168.111.65::
B. the IPv6 address of the tunnel source is ::172.168.111.65
C. the IPv6 address of the tunnel destination is 172.168.222.80::
D. the IPv6 address of the tunnel destination is ::172.168.222.80

QUESTION 5

Which of the given statements are ACCURATE about manually configured IPV4-to-IP6 tunnels and GRE tunnels? (Select two.)

A. Manually configured tunnels use the tunnel mode ipv6ip command, while GRE tunnels use the tunnel mode gre ip command.
B. Manually configured tunnels support IPv6 IGPs, while GRE tunnels do not.
C. Manually configured tunnels block IPv6 multicasts, while GRE forwards them.
D. Manually configured tunnels do not support multiple passenger protocols, while GRE tunnels support them.

QUESTION 6

Which of the given IPv6/IPv4 interoperability techniques routes both IP versions instantaneously?

A. NAT-PT
B. Dual stack
C. 6to4 tunnels
D. Teredo

QUESTION 7

Which of the given statements represent features of an automatic 6to4 tunnel through an IPv4 network? (Select all that apply.)

A. There is a NAT-PT router on either end of the tunnel.
B. There is a dual stack router on either end of the tunnel.
C. Each 6to4 site will have a /48 prefix.
D. Each 6to4 site will have a /16 prefix.
E. The IPv4 addresses of the edge routers are part of the site prefix.
F. The IPv6 addresses of the sending and receiving IPv6 hosts are part of the site prefix.

QUESTION 8

inspect the given output.

```
Router#show adjacency
Protocol      Interface      Address
IP            Serial0        10.10.10.2(2) (incomplete)
<output omitted>
```

What conceivable reason(s) can cause the state of the first entry in the adjacency table? (Select all that apply.)

A. the interface is a multipoint interface
B. the clear ip arp command was performed
C. the Layer 3 information is unknown
D. the clear adjacency command was performed

QUESTION 9

You have been notified that TCP traffic leaving an interface has been reduced to near zero, while UDP traffic is

progressively growing at the same time. What is this behavior called and what causes it?

A. jitter, caused by lack of QoS
B. latency, caused by the MTU
C. starvation, caused improper configuration of QoS queues
D. windowing, caused by network congestion

QUESTION 10

Refer to the given set of commands:

```
rtrA(config)# ipv6 unicast-routing
rtrA(config)# interface Fa0/0
rtrA(config-if)# ipv6 enable
rtrA(config-if)# ipv6 address 2001:0:1:1:D52::F3C/64
rtrA(config-if)# ip address 130.11.6.1 255.255.255.0
```

Which of the given statements is ACCURATE about the given set of commands?

A. IPv4 and IPv6 are running instantaneously on rtrA
B. The IPv4 address is translated to an IPv6 address
C. The IPv6 address is an IPv4-compatible address
D. A tunnel is created for the interoperability of the IPv4 and IPv6 addresses

QUESTION 11

Which of the given statements is ACCURATE concerning a 6to4 tunnel?

A. The IPv6 packet is encapsulated in an IPv4 packet using an IPv4 protocol type of 41.
B. The 6to4 tunnel method includes a 20-byte IPv6 header with no options and an IPv4 payload.
C. The maximum transmission unit is increased by 20 octets with the 6to4 tunnel method.
D. The IPv6 packet has its header removed and replaced with an IPv4 header with the 6to4 tunnel method.

QUESTION 12

Which of the given are valid IPv4 to IPv6 migration strategies? (Select two.)

A. DHCP
B. Tunnels
C. Dual-stack
D. Encapsulating IPv4 into IPv6

QUESTION 13

You just found that a ping packet sent from one of the devices to another took a different path in the return than it did on its way to the destination. What behavior caused this?

A. Windowing
B. Global synchronization
C. MSS
D. Asymmetric routing

QUESTION 14

In the Active Discovery phase of PPPoE, which of the given is NOT verified by the Broadband Network gateway (BNG) to prevent spoofing?

A. source MAC address
B. arriving access interface
C. PPPoE session ID
D. destination MAC address

QUESTION 15

An associate of yours configured a PPPoE connection. You have been notified by a susceptibility tester that by using a sniffer, he was able to learn the connection credentials.

What type of verification needs to your associate have configured on the connection?

A. PAP
B. 802.1x
C. CHAP
D. IPsec

QUESTION 16

You have a Frame Relay topology that is presently a hub and spoke using a single physical serial interface on the hub router with the default network type. OSPF is also running on the interface.

You execute the given command:

ip ospf network point-to-point

What could be the effect of executing this command on the serial interface of the hub router?

A. The hello interval for OSPF will change to 30 seconds
B. The dead interval for OSPF will change to 40 seconds
C. There will now be a DR election
D. The hub router needs to now be configured with a router ID

QUESTION 17

Which of the given is NOT accurate of the PPP Session Phase of PPPoE?

A. PPP options are negotiated
B. BNG sends a PPPoE Active Discovery Offer to the client
C. Verification is performed
D. Once link setup is complete, data will be transferred across the PPP link within PPPoE headers

QUESTION 18

The display is a frame relay hub-and-spoke topology with router A as the hub.

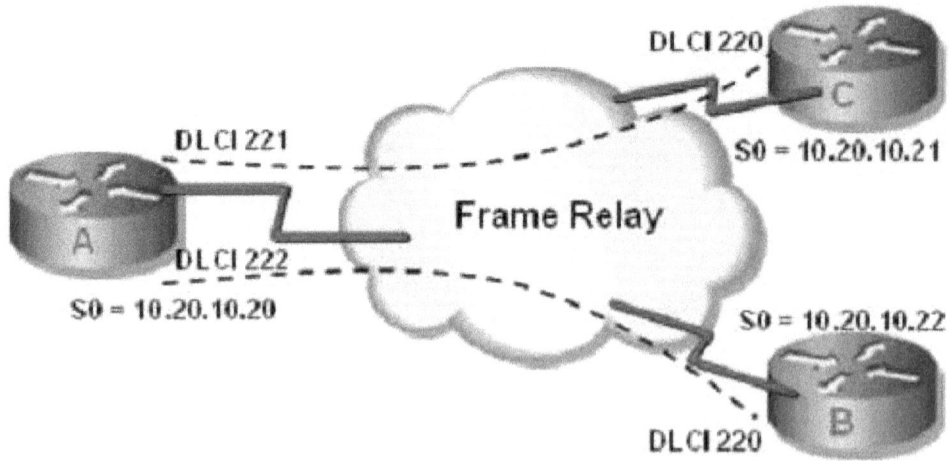

You want to use the OSPF routing protocol among all three locations. Which interface configuration commands are crucial on router A? (Select three.)

A. ip ospf network broadcast
B. ip ospf network point-to-point
C. ip ospf network point-to-multipoint
D. frame-relay map 10.20.10.21 221
E. frame-relay map 10.20.10.22 222
F. frame-relay map ip 10.20.10.21 221 broadcast
G. frame-relay map ip 10.20.10.22 222 broadcast

QUESTION 19

Which command shows only OSPF routes installed into the routing table?

A. show ip route
B. show ip ospf route
C. show ip route ospf
D. show ip ospf
E. show ip ospf database

QUESTION 20

Which commands will prevent the local router from advertising the 139.10.0.0 network out of the Ethernet 0/0 interface, while allowing all other networks to be advertised?

A. RouterA(config)router rip
RouterA(config-router)# network 10.0.0.0
RouterA(config-router)# network 139.10.0.0
RouterA(config-router)# network 199.10.10.0 RouterA(config-router)# distribute-list 10 out e0/0
RouterA(config)# access-list 10 deny 139.10.0.0 0.0.255.255 RouterA(config)# access-list 10 permit any

B. RouterA(config)router rip
RouterA(config-router)# network 10.0.0.0
RouterA(config-router)# network 139.10.0.0
RouterA(config-router)# network 199.10.10.0 RouterA(config-router)# distribute-list 10 in e0/0
RouterA(config)# access-list 10 deny 139.10.0.0 0.0.255.255 RouterA(config)# access-list 10 permit any

C. RouterA(config)# router rip RouterA(config-router)# network 10.0.0.0
RouterA(config-router)# network 139.10.0.0
RouterA(config-router)# network 199.10.10.0

RouterA(config-router)# access-group 10 out e0/0 RouterA(config)# access-list 10 deny 139.10.0.0 0.0.255.255 RouterA(config)# access-list 10 permit any

D. RouterA(config)# router rip RouterA(config-router)# network 10.0.0.0
RouterA(config-router)# network 139.10.0.0
RouterA(config-router)# network 199.10.10.0
RouterA(config)# access-list 10 deny 139.10.0.0 0.0.255.255 RouterA(config)# access-list 10 permit any
RouterA(config)# interface e0/0 RouterA(config-if)# access-group 10 out

QUESTION 21

Which of the given commands must you use to define both the feasible successors and the non-feasible successors to a given destination network?

A. show ip route eigrp
B. show ip eigrp topology
C. show ip eigrp topology all-links
D. show ip eigrp topology zero-successors

QUESTION 22
An EIGRP network is configured with default settings for all the routers, presented in the display. Traffic is not routing correctly.

What commands need to be run, and on which router must it be run?

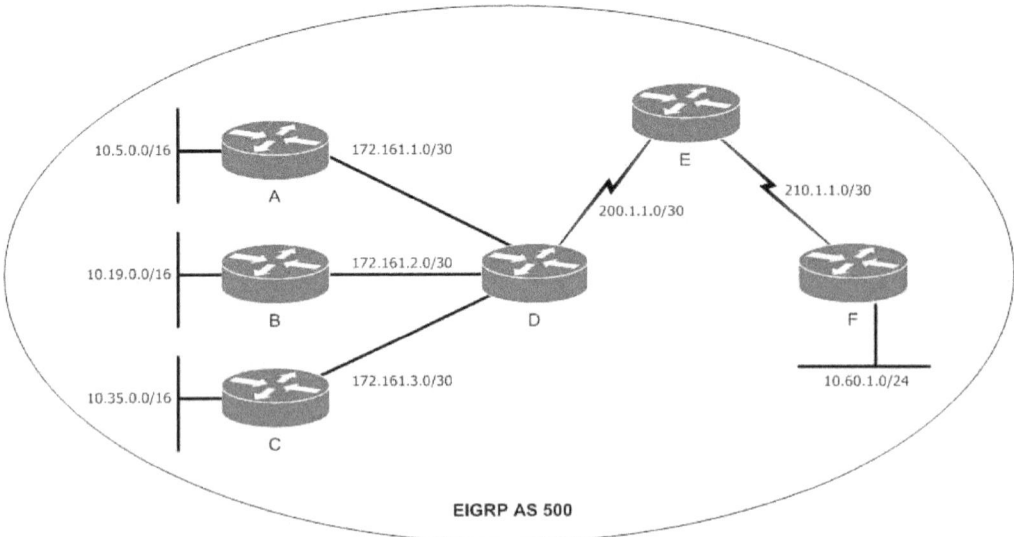

A. The ip summary-address eigrp 500 172.16.0.0.0 255.255.0.0 command must be run on Router D.
B. The ip summary-address eigrp 500 172.16.3.0.0 255.255.255.0 command must be run on Router C.
C. The no auto-summary command must be run on Routers A, B, C and F
D. The auto-summary command must be run on Router D.

QUESTION 23

Which of the given commands could reveal the K values configured on an EIGRP router?

A. debug ip eigrp
B. debug eigrp packet
C. show ip eigrp traffic
D. show ip protocols

QUESTION 24

You can use a variety of commands to verify and troubleshoot the operation of route redistribution on your network. Which command must you NOT use on routers that are overloaded?

A. trace
B. debug
C. show ip route
D. show ipx route

QUESTION 25

You manage the corporation network, as presented in the network diagram below:

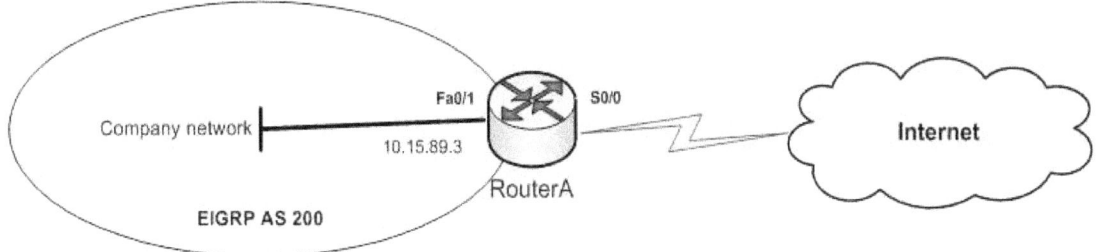

You performed the given command on RouterA:

**routerA(config)# ip route 0.0.0.0 0.0.0.0 S0/0 routerA(config)# router eigrp 200
routerA(config-router)# redistribute static metric 1000 1 255 1 1500**

Which of the given statements are ACCURATE about the given set of commands? (Select two.)

A. A static default route is created on RouterA
B. A summary default route is created on RouterA
C. The default route is redistributed into the EIGRP network
D. The default route is not advertised to the EIGRP network

QUESTION 26

Which show command displays the status of all of a router's Border Gateway Protocol (BGP) connections in a concise format?

A. show ip bgp
B. show ip bgp summary
C. show ip bgp connections
D. show ip bgp neighbor's summary

QUESTION 27

Which of the given does the show ip eigrp topology all-links command display?

A. Only feasible successors
B. Only non-feasible successors
C. Both feasible successors and non-feasible successors
D. Both successors and feasible successors

QUESTION 28

Router10 is an area system border router (ASBR). The interfaces on Router 10 are configured as below:

S 0/0   10.0.0.0/8 S0/1   172.16.0.0/8 Fa0/0   192.168.5.0/24 Fa0/1   192.168.6.0/24

You could like Router 10 to advertise the 192.168.5.0/24 and the 192.168.6.0/24 networks over OSPF in its

Type 5 link-state advertisements (LSAs). What command set could instruct the router to do this?

A. RTA10(config)# router ospf 1 RTA10(config-router)# redistribute static
B. RTA10(config)# router ospf 1
   RTA10(config-router)# redistribute connected
C. RTA10(config)# router ospf 1 RTA10(config)# redistribute connected
D. RTA10(config)# router ospf 1
   RTA10(config-router)# network 192.168.5.0 0.0.0.0 area 1
   RTA10(config-router)# network 192.168.6.0 0.0.0.0 area 1

QUESTION 29

Refer to the given partial output of the show ip bgp neighbors command:

```
rtrA# show ip bgp neighbors 172.161.81.7

BGP neighbor is 172.161.81.7, remote AS 151, external link
BGP version 45, remote router ID 10.8.22.4
BGP state = Established, up for 01:45:55
Last read 00:10:17, last write 00:10:17, hold time is 180, keepalive interval is 60 seconds
Neighbor capabilities:
Route refresh: advertised and received(old & new)
Graceful Restart Capabilty: advertised and received
Address family IPv4 Unicast: advertised and received
!
!
!
Connections established 8; dropped 6
Last reset 00:10:17, due to Peer closed the session
Connection state is ESTAB, I/O status: 1, unread input bytes: 0
Connection is ECN Disabled
Local host: 10.167.121.90., Local port: 112
Foreign host: 172.161.81.7, Foreign port: 6781
<output omitted>
```

Which of the given can NOT be defined from the given output? (Select all that apply.)

A. The ASN of rtrA
B. The ASN of 172.161.81.7
C. The best paths among rtrA and the 172.161.81.7 neighbor
D. The RID of the 172.161.81.7 neighbor
E. The status of the connection among rtrA and 172.161.81.7

QUESTION 30

inspect the display.

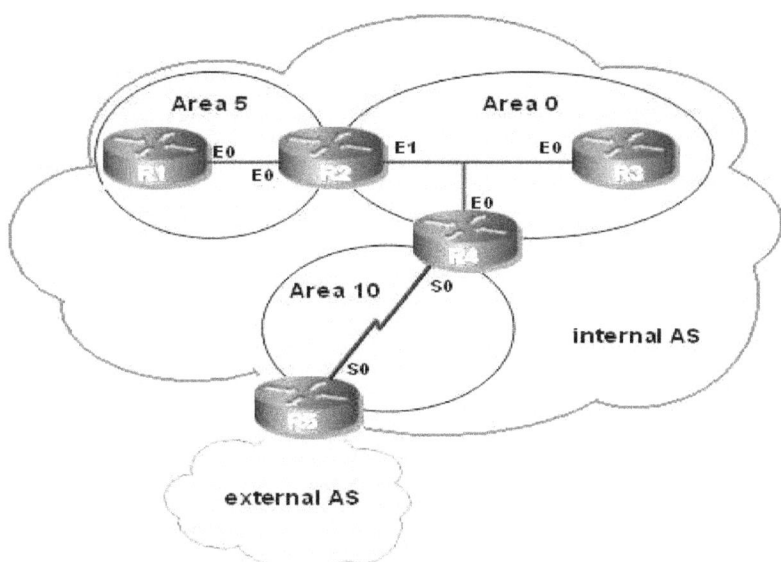

You are asked to configure the routers R1, R2, R3, and R4. (Refer to the IP addressing table below.) Which configuration command series is crucial to ensure that router R1 will NOT be receiving Type 3, 4, or 5 LSAs?

R1 interface E0 - 172.31.200.1/21 R2 interface E0 - 172.31.200.2/21 R2 interface E1 - 172.31.208.2/21 R3 interface E0 - 172.31.208.3/21

A. R1(config)# router ospf 5

   R1(config-router)# area 5 stub
   R1(config-router)# network 172.31.200.0 0.0.7.255 area 5
B. R2(config)# router ospf 5
   R2(config-router)# area 5 stub no-summary
   R2(config-router)# network 172.31.200.0 0.0.7.255 area 5 R1(config)# router ospf 5
   R1(config-router)area 5 stub
   R1(config-router)# network 172.31.200.0 0.0.7.255 area 5
C. R1(config)# router ospf 10 R1(config-router)# area 5 stub
   R1(config-router)# network 172.31.200.0 255.255.248.0 area 5
D. R2(config)# router ospf 10
   R2(config-router)# area 5 stub no-summary
   R2(config-router)# network 172.31.200.0 255.255.248.0 area 5

QUESTION 31

Which EIGRP packet type is sent as a multicast when a new route is found, and sent as a unicast to synchronize topology tables when neighbors initialize?

A. ACK
B. Hello
C. Update
D. Replies
E. Queries

QUESTION 32

Your corporation has a policy of creating all configurations in text files, checking the files, and then applying the configurations to the devices. Your assistant has presented you with the given partial configuration that she plans to execute on a router:

```
interface S0/0/1
ipv6 address 2001:610:FFFF:1::1/64 ipv6 ospf 100 area 0

ipv6 router ospf 100 router-id 10.1.1.6
```

The configuration is supposed to accomplish the given: Enable IPv6 routing
- Assign a router ID
- Assign an IPv6 address to the interface Place the interface in OSPF area 0
-

Which step does this configuration NOT complete?

A. Enable IPv6 routing
B. Assign a router ID
C. Assign an IPv6 address to the interface
D. Place the interface in OSPF area 0

QUESTION 33

Which show command displays entries in a router's Border Gateway Protocol (BGP) table?

A. show ip bgp
B. show ip bgp table
C. show ip bgp topology
D. show ip bgp summary

QUESTION 34

Corporation A in recent times acquired Corporation B and the network infrastructures are being merged. Both organizations used non-overlapping worldwidely unique network addressing but different Interior Gateway Protocols (IGPs). Initially, multiple WAN links will connect the two organizations. Corporation A will maintain its core routing protocol, and Corporation B's routing protocol will be the edge routing protocol. Two-way redistribution will be used to ensure full network routing capability.

What additional routing configuration must be performed to prevent routing loops and suboptimal routing?

A. Manually configure static routes.
B. Manually configure default routes.
C. Manually adjust the administrative distances.
D. Manually adjust the local preference attribute.

QUESTION 35

Refer to the given table:

Parameters ⇩	Values ⇨	Path 1	Path2	Path3
Weight		500	500	500
LOCAL_PREF		150	150	150
Local Originate Source Command		Redistribute	Redistribute	Network
AS_PATH		50 20 40	20 30 40	10 20 ?
Origin Type		IGP	IGP	IGP
MED		300	250	200
Protocol type		iBGP	iBGP	iBGP

Path1, Path2, and Path3 are the available routes among routers A and B. The bgp always-compare med command is performed for all three routes.

What must be the value for the missing ASN (represented by a question mark in the table) so that Path3 becomes the best path among routers A and B based on their MED values?

A. 10
B. 20
C. 30
D. 40

QUESTION 36

Refer to the given display that shows four Cisco routers named rtr1, rtr2, rtr3, and rtr4:

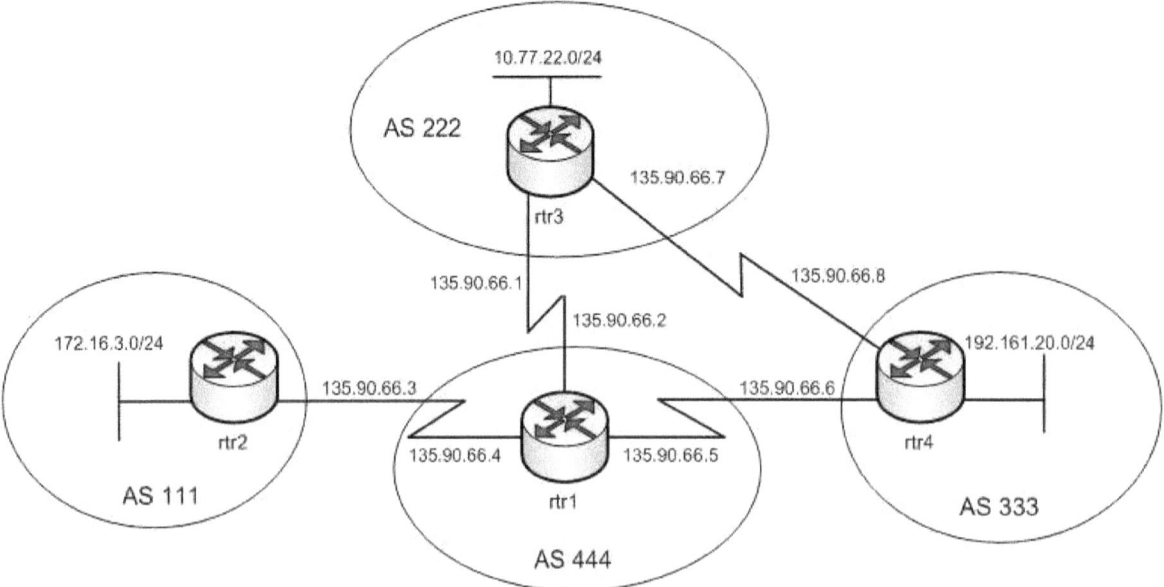

The routers rtr2, rtr3, and rtr4 are eBGP peers of rtr1. In addition, rtr3 and rtr4 are also eBGP peers.

You want to execute the given necessitates on rtr1: The first attribute to select the best path is used.
- Advertisements about 10.77.22.0/24 sent by rtr4 will be chosen over the advertisements sent by rtr3.

Which of the given commands must be included in the execution plan for rtr1 to achieve the desired results? (Each option is a part of the solution. Select all that apply.)

A. neighbor 135.90.66.1 route-map set_weight out
B. neighbor 135.90.66.6 route-map set_weight in
C. route-map set_weight deny 10
D. match ip-address 1
E. set metric 100
F. set weight 100

QUESTION 37

Consider the given output of the show ip bgp summary command:

```
RouterA# show ip bgp summary
BGP router identifier 10.1.1.1, local AS number 210
BGP table version is 45, main routing table version 45
7 network entries using 1715 bytes of memory
9 path entries using 3318 bytes of memory
15 BGP path attribute entries using 156 bytes of memory
1 multipath network entries and 4 multipath paths
1 BGP AS-PATH entries using 50 bytes of memory
3 BGP community entries using 150 bytes of memory
0 BGP route-map cache entries using 0 bytes of memory
0 BGP filter-list cache entries using 0 bytes of memory
3 received paths for inbound soft reconfiguration
BGP using 10249 total bytes of memory
Dampening enabled. 4 history paths, 0 dampened paths
BGP activity 7/570 prefixes, 10/1 paths, scan interval 15 secs

Neighbor V AS MsgRcvd MsgSent TblVer InQ OutQ Up/Down State/PfxRcd
10.1.1.1 4 950 78 80 45 0 0 01:53:41 OPENSENT
10.2.1.1 4 950 23 22 45 0 0 00:10:32 15
10.3.1.1 4 950 30 44 45 0 0 00:24:11 IDLE
10.4.1.1 4 950 12 56 45 0 0 00:56:06 ACTIVE
10.5.1.1 4 950 67 67 45 0 0 01:17:34 OPENCONFIRM
```

Which of the given neighbors have an established connection with RouterA? A. 10.1.1.1
B. 10.2.1.1
C. 10.3.1.1
D. 10.4.1.1
E. 10.5.1.1

QUESTION 38

Router 5 has four interfaces. The networks hosted on each interface are as follows:

Fa0/1   192.168.5.4/29
Fa0/2   192.168.6.0/24
Fa0/3   192.168.7.0/24
S0/0   172.16.5.0/24

You execute the given commands on the router:

```
Router5(config)# router bgp 20
Router5(config-router)# network 192.168.5.0
Router5(config-router)# network 192.168.6.0
Router5(config-router)# network 192.168.7.0
Router5(config-router)# network 172.16.5.0
Router5(config-router)# neighbor 172.16.5.2 remote-as 50
Router5(config-router)# aggregate-address 192.168.5.0 255.255.252.0
```

After this command sequence is performed, what routes will be present in the routing table of the router at 172.16.5.2? (Select all that apply.)

A. 192.168.5.4/29
B. 172.16.5.0/24
C. 192.168.6.0/24
D. 192.168.7.0/24
E. none of these will be present
F. only network addresses beginning with 192 will be present

QUESTION 39

You manage the EIGRP subnet in your organization. You have enabled EIGRP for IPv6 on all the routers in the EIGRP AS 355 using the given commands on all the routers:
- The ipv6 unicast-routing command in worldwide configuration mode The interface command in worldwide
- configuration mode
- The ipv6 enable command in interface configuration mode The ipv6 eigrp command in interface
- configuration mode The ipv6 router eigrp command in worldwide configuration mode The eigrp router-id
- command in worldwide configuration mode
.
During verification, you discover that EIGRP for IPv6 is not running on the routers. Which of the given must be

done to fix the issue?

A. The ipv6 address command must be performed in interface configuration mode.
B. The ipv6 address command must be performed in router configuration mode.
C. The eigrp router-id command must be performed in interface configuration mode.
D. The eigrp router-id command must be performed in router configuration mode.

QUESTION 40

Router R2 operates in a broadcast, multi-access network. inspect the given output of the show ip ospf neighbor command.

```
R2# show ip ospf neighbor fa0/1

NeighborID PRI State Dead Time Address Interface
1.1.1.1 1 2WAY/DROTHER 00:00:13 192.168.5.6 FastEthetnet 0/1
2.2.2.2 1 2WAY/DROTHER 00:00:04 192.168.5.10 FastEthetnet 0/1
3.3.3.3 1 2WAY/DROTHER 00:00:47 192.168.5.116 FastEthetnet 0/1
4.4.4.4 1 FULL/BDR 00:00:36 192.168.5.107 FastEthetnet 0/1
5.5.5.5 1 FULL/DR 00:00:49 192.168.5.165 FastEthetnet 0/1
```

Based on the output, with which routers can R2 establish a full adjacency?

A. the neighbor at 192.168.5.6
B. the neighbor at 192.168.5.10
C. the neighbor at 192.168.5.116
D. the neighbor at 192.168.5.107

QUESTION 41

RouterA and RouterB are both in OSPF area 2, and RouterA is connected directly to the backbone. Their router IDs are presented below:

RouterA - 165.165.20.15
RouterB - 165.165.10.12

Which commands must be performed on RouterA and RouterB to create a virtual link among the two routers?

A. RouterA(config-router)# area 2 virtual-link 165.165.10.12 RouterB(config-router)# area 2 virtual-link 165.165.20.15
B. RouterA(config-router)# area 2 virtual-link 165.165.10.12 RouterB(config-router)# area 0 virtual-link 165.165.20.15
C. RouterA(config-router)# area 0 virtual-link 165.165.20.15 RouterB(config-router)# area 2 virtual-link 165.165.10.12
D. RouterA(config-router)# area 0 virtual-link 165.165.10.12 RouterB(config-router)# area 0 virtual-link 165.165.20.15

QUESTION 42

Based on the given partial output of the show ip ospf database command, which router roles(s) is Router7 performing? (Select all that apply.)

```
Router7# show ip ospf database
OSPF Router with ID(192.168.5.8) (Process ID 1)

Router Link States(Area 0)
Link ID ADV Router Age Seq# Checksum Link count
192.168.5.8  192.168.5.8  1381 0x8000010D 0xEF60 2
192.168.5.11 192.168.5.11 1460 0x800002FE 0xEB3D 4
192.168.5.12 192.168.5.12 2027 0x80000090 0x875D 3
192.168.5.27 192.168.5.27 1323 0x800001D6 0x12CC 3

Net Link States(Area 0)
Link ID ADV Router Age Seq# Checksum
172.16.9.27 192.168.5.27 1323 0x8000005B 0xA8EE
172.17.9.11 192.168.5.11 1461 0x8000005B 0x7AC
<<output omitted>>

Router Link States(Area 2)
Link ID ADV Router Age Seq# Checksum Link count
192.168.5.8  192.168.5.8  1381 0x8000010D 0xEF60 2
192.168.5.13 192.168.5.11 1460 0x800002FE 0xEB3D 4

Net Link States(Area 2)
Link ID ADV Router Age Seq# Checksum
172.16.9.27 192.168.5.8  1323 0x8000005B 0xA8EE
172.17.9.11 192.168.5.11 1461 0x8000005B 0x7AC
<<output omitted>>
```

A. ABR
B. ASBR
C. BR
D. IR

QUESTION 43

inspect the diagram below:

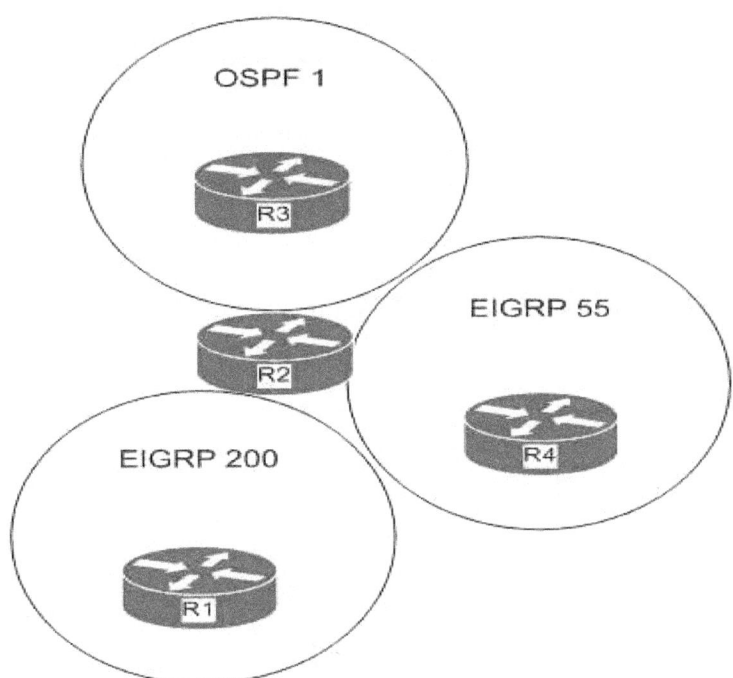

Based on the diagram and the given partial output from Router R2, which networks will be present in the routing table of Router R1?

```
R2# show run
!
router eigrp 200
     network 192.168.5.0
     redistribute eigrp 55


router eigrp 55
     network 10.0.0.0

router ospf 1
     redistribute eigrp 200
     default-metric 50
     network 172.50.0.0
```

A. 192.168.5.0
B. 10.0.0.0
C. 172.50.0.0
D. 192.168.5.0 and 10.0.0.0

QUESTION 44

Refer to the given diagram of an OSPF network.

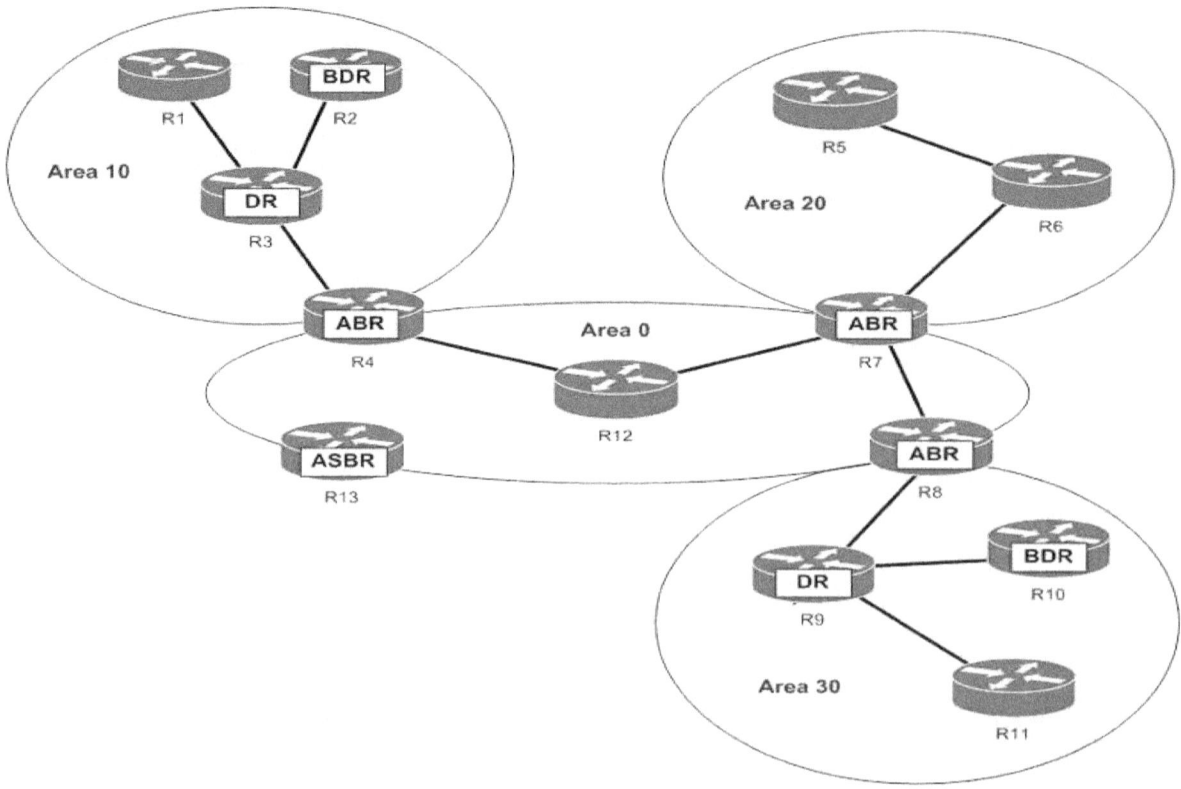

Which of the given routers generate network link advertisements (NLA)? (Select all that apply.)

A. R3
B. R4
C. R7
D. R8
E. R9
F. R13

QUESTION 45

You instructed your assistant to configure redistribution of OSPF routes into EIGRP on Router 9. The routes are not being advertised to EIGRP and you are troubleshooting the issue. The EIGRP process ID is 100 and the OSPF process ID is 20. When you ask your assistant what commands were performed, you are presented the given:

Router9(config)# router eigrp 100 Router9(config-router)# redistribute ospf 20

What is the issue?
A. no metric was configured
B. the process IDs are incorrect
C. the redistribute command is performed at the interface configuration prompt
D. the redistribute command is performed at the worldwide configuration prompt

QUESTION 46

inspect the display by pressing the Display(s) button.

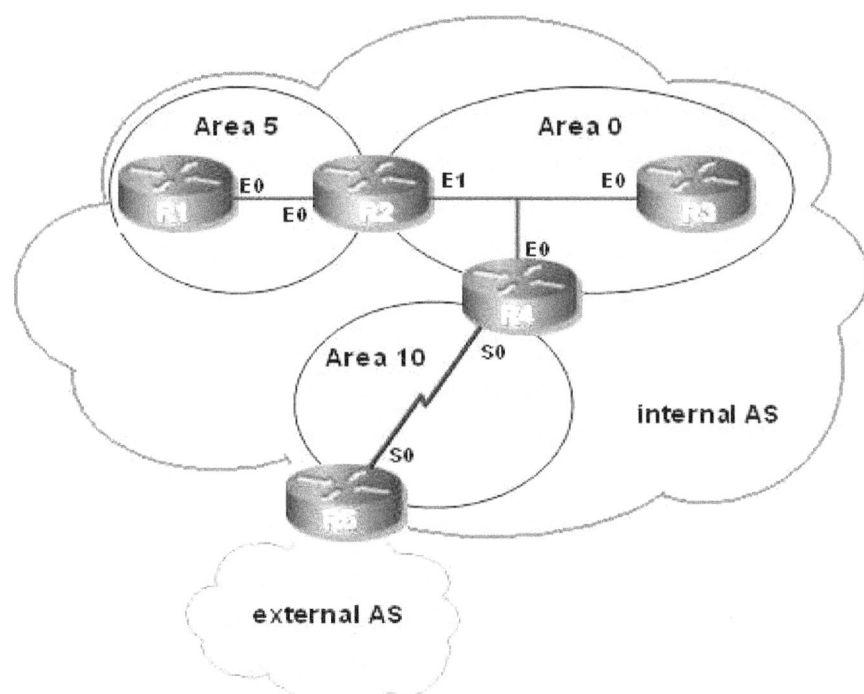

You are to configure R1 to belong to area 5. This area does not accept routes from the external AS or summary routes from any other internal areas. Refer to the IP addressing below.

R1 - int E0 - 192.168.5.1/24 R2 - int E0 - 192.168.5.2/24 R2 - int E1 - 192.168.0.2/24 R3 - int E0 - 192.168.0.3/24

Which configuration commands are crucial to correctly configure R1?

A. R1(config)# router ospf 10

R1(config-router)# area 5 no-summary stub
R1(config-router)# network 192.168.5.0 0.0.0.255 area 5

B. R1(config)# router ospf 5 R1(config-router)# area 5 stub
R1(config-router)# network 192.168.5.0 0.0.0.255 area 5

C. R1(config)# router ospf 10 R1(config-router)# area 5 stub
R1(config-router)# network 192.168.5.0 255.255.255.0 area 5

D. R1(config)# router ospf 5
R1(config-router)# area 5 stub no-summary
R1(config-router)# network 192.168.5.0 255.255.255.0 area 5

QUESTION 47

You are the network administrator for a large software organization. You designed the LAN in the organization's main building for connecting the internal LAN to a WAN as presented below:

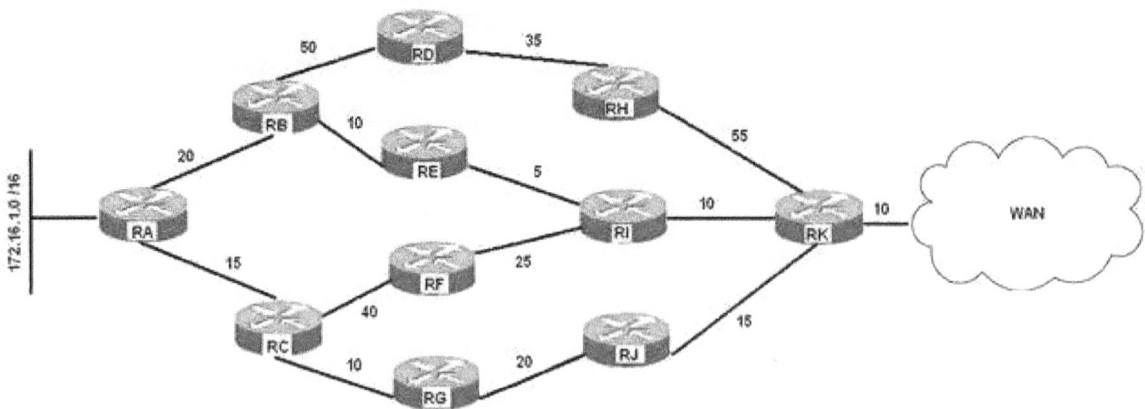

You have configured EIGRP with the variance parameter set to 3 on all the routers to enable unequal load balancing from the 172.16.1.0 network to the WAN. The delay configured on each of the routers is presented in the LAN diagram, and the K values are set as follows:

K1 = 0
K2 = 0
K3 = 1
K4 = 0
K5 = 0

Which of the given paths are entered into the routing tables as a result of the unequal load balancing configured on the routers? (Select all that apply.)

A. RA-RB-RD-RH-RK
B. RA-RB-RE-RI-RK
C. RA-RC-RF-RI-RK
D. RA-RC-RG-RJ-RK

QUESTION 48

OSPF area border routers (ABRs) advertise a default route to stub and totally stubby areas.

Which command is the BEST command to configure a cost of 25 for the default route advertised to area 1?

A. Router(config-router)# area 1 cost 25
B. Router(config-router)# area 1 default 25
C. Router(config-router)# area 1 default-cost 25
D. Router(config-router)# area 1 default-route-cost 25

QUESTION 49

You need to manually assign IPv6 addresses to the interfaces on an IPv6-enabled router. While assigning addresses, you need to ensure that the addresses participate in neighbor discovery and in stateless auto-configuration process on a physical link.

Which of the given addresses can be appointed to the interfaces? A. FEC0:0:0:1::1/64

B. FE80::260:3EFF:FE11:6770/10

C. 2001:0410:0:1:0:0:0:1/64
D. 2002:500E:2301:1:20D:BDFF:FE99:F559/64

QUESTION 50

You are configuring EIGRP on a spoke router in a hub-and-spoke topology. In an effort to keep the routing table small, the hub router has been configured to send only a default route to the remote routers.

What command could you use on the spoke routers to enable them to send only connected and summary routes to the hub router, and prevent the hub router from sending a query to the spoke router when a route is lost elsewhere?

A. eigrp stub
B. eigrp stub static
C. eigrp passive
D. eigrp stub receive-only

QUESTION 51

Which conditions will prevent two EIGRP routers from becoming neighbors? (Select two.)

A. Their K-values do not match.
B. Their hold times do not match.
C. Their AS numbers do not match.
D. Their hello intervals do not match.

QUESTION 52

The display contains portions of RouterA's BGP configuration and IP routing table.

```
!
router bgp 65100
neighbor 192.168.12.34 remote-as 65101
network 172.16.0.0
no synchronization
auto-summary
!

RouterA# show ip route
:
O    172.16.16.0/24 [110/128] via 10.1.2.3 00:24:16, Serial0
O    172.16.24.0/24 [110/144] via 10.1.2.3 00:24:16, Serial1
:
```

Which IP network addresses, that were not learned using BGP, will be present in BGP advertisements from

RouterA? A. 172.16.0.0/16
B. 172.16.16.0/24
C. 172.16.24.0/20
D. No IGP networks will be advertised because synchronization is disabled.

QUESTION 53

You are configuring BGP speakers RouterA and RouterB to authenticate one another. The given conditions take
- place: RouterA has an IP address of 192.168.5.3
- RouterB has an IP address of 192.168.5.2 Both routers reside in AS 6550.

Which of the given commands will result in successful verification?

A. neighbor 192.168.5.2 password routera performed on RouterA neighbor 192.168.5.3 password routerb performed on RouterB
B. neighbor 192.168.5.2 password routerb performed on RouterA neighbor 192.168.5.3 password routera performed on RouterB
C. neighbor 192.168.5.2 password routera performed on RouterA neighbor 192.168.5.3 password routera performed on RouterB
D. neighbor 192.168.5.2 password routera performed on RouterA
E. neighbor 192.168.5.2 password routerb performed on RouterB

QUESTION 54

With respect to modifying an OSPF router ID to a loopback address, which of the given statements are accurate?

A. OSPF is not as reliable if a loopback interface is configured.
B. Using a loopback address avoids wasting an additional IP address.
C. A loopback interface is not always active, and it can go "down" like a real interface.
D. The loopback address does not automatically appear in the routing table of neighboring OSPF routers, so it cannot be pinged from other routers unless you include it with a network statement on the router local to the loopback interface.

QUESTION 55

Which statements in regards to route filtering are accurate? (Select two.)

A. Network security is the primary role of route filtering.
B. If no route filter take places for an interface, the packet is processed normally.
C. Route filtering on an interface cannot filter routes that originate from the same router.
D. The distribute-list command enables the administrator to filter redistributed routes.
E. The network keyword of the passive-interface command enables you identify the routes to advertise.

QUESTION 56

By default, how often are EIGRP hello packets sent on a LAN?

A. 5 seconds
B. 10 seconds
C. 30 seconds
D. 60 seconds

QUESTION 57

Which of the given commands allows a Cisco router to obtain an IP address from a DHCP server?

A. Router(config-if)# ip address dhcp
B. Router(config)# ip address dhcp
C. Router(dhcp-config)# ip address dhcp
D. Router(config)# address dhcp
E. Router(dhcp-config)# address dhcp

QUESTION 58

Which command shows a list of neighboring routers, their priorities, and their current state?

A. show ip ospf
B. show ip protocol
C. show ip ospf database
D. show ip ospf neighbor [detail]

QUESTION 59

Which of the given statements is ACCURATE about the communication take placering among rtrA and rtrB in the given display?

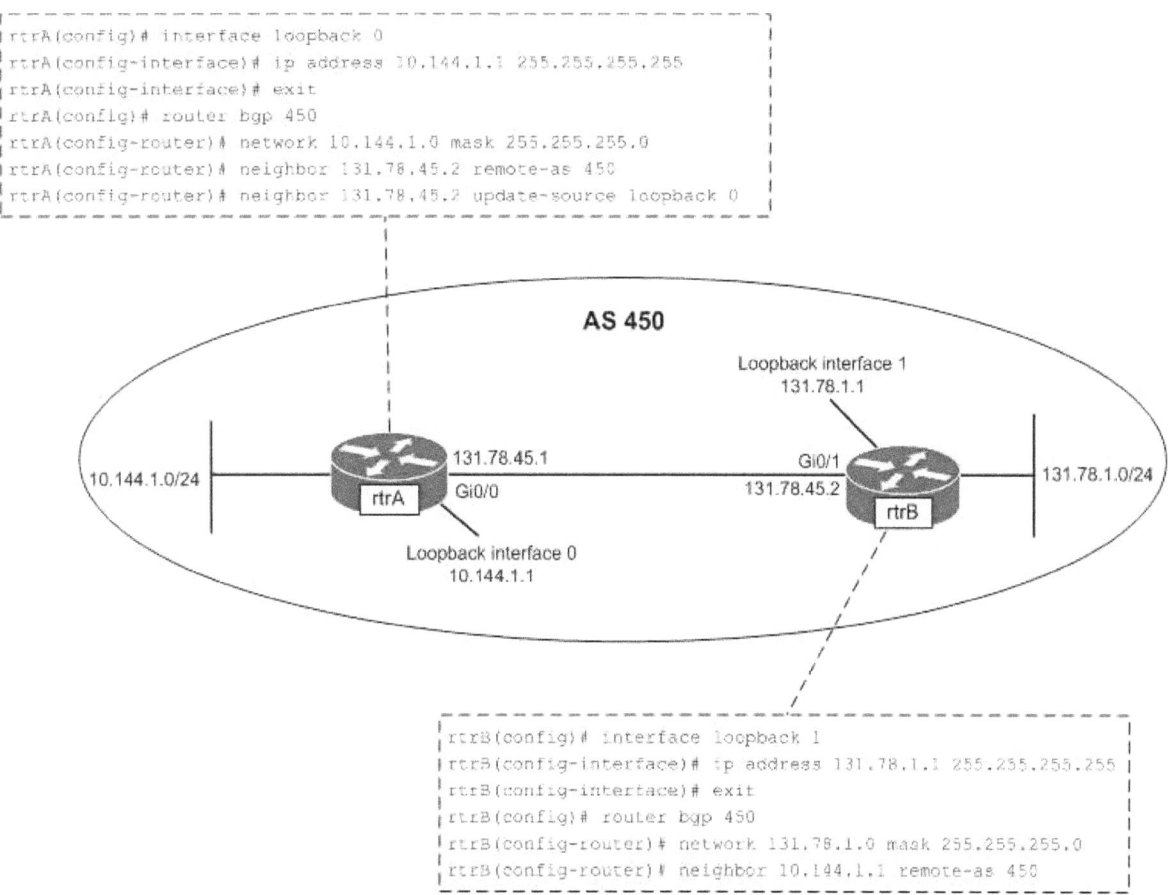

A. The only loopback interface used in the communication is the loopback 0 interface of rtrA.
B. The only loopback interface used in the communication is the loopback 1 interface of rtrB.
C. Both loopback 0 and loopback 1 interfaces are used for the communication among rtrA and rtrB.
D. Neither loopback 0 nor loopback 1 interface is used for the communication among rtrA and rtrB.

QUESTION 60

Which command can you use to specify that network 208.15.208.0 belongs to OSPF area 0?

A. router(config)# network 208.15.208.0 area 0
B. router(config-if)# ip ospf area 0
C. router(config)# network 208.15.208.0 255.255.255.0 area 0
D. router(config-router)# network 208.15.208.0 0.0.0.255 area 0

QUESTION 61

Consider the partial output of the show ip bgp command:

```
RouterA# show ip bgp
BGP table version is 89, local router ID is 200.17.34.15
.
.
Network Next Hop Metric LocPrf Weight Path
*>i 10.62.7.0 10.62.7.78 0 100 0 1 i
*>e 192.177.1.0 10.62.7.115 100 75 50 1 2 3 5 i
h  61.80.3.0 10.62.7.44 0 100 0 1 2 3 5 9 i
*>i 200.17.56.0 200.17.56.101 0 100 0 i
*>  200.17.34.0 0.0.0.0 0 100 32768 i
```

Which of the given statements are ACCURATE about the given output? (Select all that apply.)

A. The 10.62.7.0 route is learned by the router through an iBGP neighbor.
B. All five routes have been originated by an IGP.
C. The router is aware of the best path for the 61.80.3.0 destination.
D. There are four AS among the router and the 192.177.1.0 subnet.

QUESTION 62

Which of the given statements is NOT accurate about BGP peers?

A. eBGP peers use TCP to communicate
B. eBGP peers use port 179 by default
C. eBGP peers do not update the AS_Path attribute before sending updates to another eBGP peer
D. iBGP peers do not update the AS_Path attribute before sending updates to an iBGP peer

QUESTION 63

Which of the given commands configures an SNMP host to authenticate a user by username and send clear text notifications, the receipt of which will be acknowledged by the receiver?

A. Router(config)# snmp-server host 192.168.5.5 informs version 3 noauth CISCO
B. Router(config)# snmp-server host 192.168.5.5 traps version 3 auth CISCO
C. Router(config)# snmp-server host 192.168.5.5 informs version 2c CISCO
D. Router(config)# snmp-server host 192.168.5.5 informs version 3 authpriv CISCO

QUESTION 64

Consider the given commands:

```
RouterA(config)# router ospf 10
RouterA(config-router)# redistribute eigrp 20 metric 30
```

What does the value of 30 represent?

A. It identifies the seed metric associated with OSPF routes that are redistributed into EIGRP.
B. It identifies the seed metric associated with EIGRP routes that are redistributed into OSPF.
C. It identifies the amount that the take placering EIGRP metric will increment as it is redistributed into OSPF.
D. It specifies that routes that contain metrics of less than 30 will be redistributed from OSPF into EIGRP.

QUESTION 65

If the given protocols are redistributed into OSPF, which protocol will receive a metric of 1 if none is specified, rather than the default metric of 20?

A. EIGRP
B. RIP
C. IGRP
D. BGP

QUESTION 66

You need to configure eBGP on the rtrA and rtrB routers, as presented in the given image:

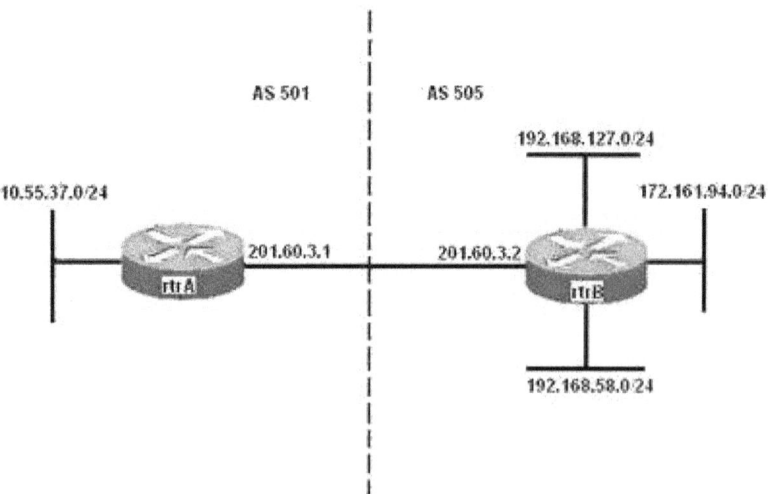

You have configured eBGP on rtrA through the given commands:

```
rtrA(config)# router bgp 501
rtrA(config)# neighbor 201.60.3.2 remote-as 505
```

While configuring eBGP on rtrB, you need to ensure that updates about the 192.168.58.0/24 and the 192.168.127.0/24 subnets are sent to rtrA with a metric of 300.

In addition, rtrB must send updates about the 172.161.94.0/24 subnet are sent with a metric of 500.

Which of the given set of commands could NOT be part of the set used to correctly configure eBGP on rtrB?

A. access-list 1 permit 192.168.0.0 0.0.255.255
   access-list 2 permit 172.161.94.0 0.0.0.255
   router bgp 505
   neighbor 201.60.3.1 remote-as 501
   neighbor 201.60.3.1 route-map change_parameters in
B. access-list 1 permit 192.168.0.0 0.0.255.255
   access-list 2 permit 172.161.94.0 0.0.0.255
   router bgp 505
   neighbor 201.60.3.1 remote-as 501
   neighbor 201.60.3.1 route-map change_parameters out
C. route-map change_parameters permit 10 match ip-address 2
   set metric 500
D. route-map change_parameters permit 20 match ip-address 1
   set metric 300

QUESTION 67

For a non-ISP autonomous system (AS), which combination of two conditions will require redistribution from BGP into Interior Gateway Protocol (IGP)? (Select two.)

A. All routers run BGP.
B. Not all routers run BGP.
C. No knowledge of external routes is crucial inside the AS.
D. Routers inside the AS require knowledge of external routes.

QUESTION 68

Which command can you use to display information about OSPF virtual links?

A. debug ip ospf adj
B. show ip ospf [process-id]
C. show ip ospf virtual-links
D. show ip ospf border-routers

QUESTION 69

View the sample output of the debug ip eigrp command.

```
IP-EIGRP: Processing incoming REPLY packet
IP-EIGRP: Int 10.20.0.0/16 M 4294967295 - 1657856 4294967295 SM 4294967295 - 1657856 4294967295
IP-EIGRP: Int 65.0.0.0/8 M 4294967295 - 1657856 4294967295 SM 4294967295 - 1657856 4294967295
IP-EIGRP: Int 130.10.0.0/16 M 4294967295 - 1657856 4294967295 SM 4294967295 - 1657856 4294967295
```

What is the significance of the number 4294967295 as presented in the output?

A. It represents the unreachable metric for EIGRP.
B. It represents the administrative distance for EIGRP.
C. It represents a reachable metric for the given network.
D. It represents one of the link features that EIGRP uses to calculate the metric.

QUESTION 70

The network administrator has configured router R2 to redistribute a newly installed EIGRP network into their core OSPF network. The redistributed networks and subnets are not properly appearing in the routing tables of the other routers. The given output displays partial configuration for router R2:

```
router ospf 10
redistribute eigrp 50 metric 100 metric-type 1
network 192.16.31.0 0.0.0.255
```

What two modifications could correct the issue? (Select two.)

A. Change the EIGRP AS number from 50 to 10
B. Change the AS number specified for OSPF to 50
C. Add the command network 10.0.0.0 0.0.0.255
D. Add the command network 10.0.0.0 255.255.255.0
E. Add the level-1-2 keyword to the redistribute command
F. Add the subnets keyword to the redistribute command
G. Change the command network 192.16.31.0 0.0.0.255 to include the area keyword and value

QUESTION 71

A neighboring EIGRP router fails. Its advertised distance (AD) to network 10.10.10.0 was 2 and the feasible distance (FD) was 3.

Which route will be used to route packets destined for network 10.10.10.0 if the other routes have the given feasible and advertised distances respectively to the destination network?

A. FD-6AD-3
B. FD-4AD-1
C. FD-5AD-3
D. FD-4AD-3

QUESTION 72

You have two routers connected to each other that are both running the EIGRP protocol. The routers have built a neighbor relationship and are exchanging routing information. You execute the given command on the EIGRP process on Router 1:

router1(config)# router eigrp 100 router1(config-router)# passive-interface

What will be the effect of this command?

A. Only routing advertisements from Router 1 to Router 2 will be prevented.
B. Only router advertisements to and from Router 1 will be prevented.
C. All hellos and routing updates will be prevented, and the neighbor relationship among Router 1 and Router 2 will be broken.
D. Hellos will be prevented, but routing updates will continue to be sent out.

QUESTION 73

What does the passive-interface command do when execute with RIP? (Select two.)

A. Allows an interface to receive routing update traffic
B. Prevents an interface from sending routing update traffic
C. Prevents an interface from sending any normal data traffic
D. Allows an interface to receive normal data traffic
E. Disables a router interface
F. Places a router interface in standby mode

QUESTION 74

As the network administrator, you need to develop a verification plan for an OSPF network. The OSPF network has several area routers, area border routers (ABRs), and autonomous system boundary routers (ASBRs).

Which LSA types must you expect ABRs to generate while verifying the OSPF network? (Select two.)

A. Type 4
B. Type 3
C. Type 2
D. Type 5

QUESTION 75

inspect the display.

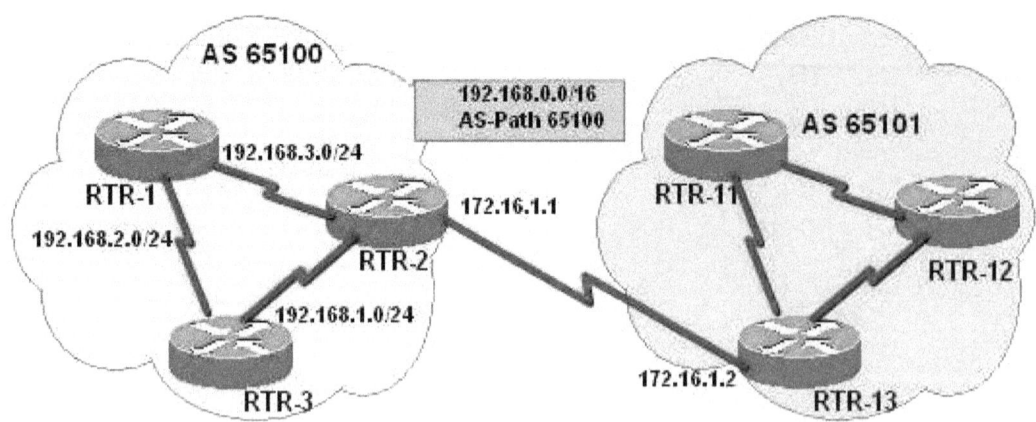

You have defined that RTR2 is not advertising the CIDR summary address 192.168.0.0 to the other routers in AS 65100.

Which set of configuration commands will enable the BGP router RTR2 to announce the network prefix 192.168.0.0/16 to the other routers in the AS 65100?

A. router bgp 65100
   neighbor 172.16.1.2 remote-as 65100
   neighbor 192.168.3.2 remote-as 65100
   network 192.168.3.0
B. router bgp 65100
   neighbor 172.16.1.2 remote-as 65101
   neighbor 192.168.3.2 remote-as 65100
   network 192.168.0.0
C. router bgp 65100
   neighbor 172.16.1.2 remote-as 65100

   neighbor 192.168.3.2 remote-as 65100
   network 192.168.0.0 mask 255.255.0.0
   ip route 192.0.0.0 255.0.0.0 null 0
D. router bgp 65100
   neighbor 172.16.1.2 remote-as 65101
   neighbor 192.168.3.2 remote-as 65100
   network 192.168.0.0 mask 255.255.0.0
   ip route 192.168.0.0 255.255.0.0 null 0

QUESTION 76

Which show command displays detailed information about a router's BGP connections to neighboring routers?

A. show ip bgp
B. show ip bgp summary
C. show ip bgp neighbors
D. show ip bgp connections

QUESTION 77

You have configured OSPF on your network and enabled route summarization on an area border router (ABR) with the given command:

Router(config-router)# area 3 range 165.164.8.0 255.255.248.0

What does the 3 specify in this command?

A. The ID of the OSPF backbone
B. The number of networks summarized in the area
C. The ID of the area about which routes will be summarized
D. The ID of the area to which the summary route information will be sent

QUESTION 78

Which of the given commands is used to verify the link-local, worldwide unicast, and multicast addresses of an IPv6 router?

A. show ipv6 neighbors (only link-local addresses)
B. show ipv6 route
C. show ipv6 protocols
D. show ipv6 interface

QUESTION 79

You performed the given commands to assign an IPv6 link-local address to the Fa0/0 interface of the R1 router:

`R1(config)# interface Fa0/0 R1(config-if)# ipv6 ospf 1 area 1`

When you performed the show running-config command on the R1 router, you observed that OSPF for IPv6 is

not running on the router. Which of the given commands must be added to the interface configuration?

A. ipv6 router ospf
B. ipv6 enable
C. ipv6 ospf neighbor
D. ipv6 ospf cost

QUESTION 80

Consider the given diagram. All PVCs are active.

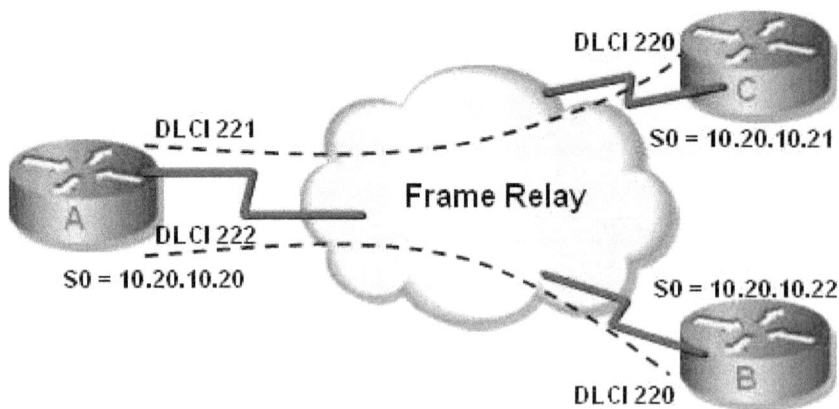

If the partial output of the show ip ospf neighbor command performed on Router A is as follows, which of the given statements is ACCURATE?

```
RouterA# show ip ospf neighbor

Neighbor ID Pri State Dead Time Address Interface
1.1.1.1 1 FULL/DROTHER 00:00:13 10.20.10.21 Serial0 2.2.2.2 1 FULL/DR 00:00:51
10.20.10.22 Serial0
```

A. Router C and Router B will fail to have all OSPF routes in their tables.
B. All routing tables will be populated correctly.
C. Router A will be the DR.
D. Router C will be the DR.

QUESTION 81

When configuring a DMVPN solution, which of the given technologies makes it conceivable for the spoke routers to use dynamic IP addressing?

A. IPsec
B. mGRE
C. NHRP
D. Dynamic routing protocols

QUESTION 82

The given configuration was applied to the router R66:

```
R66# show running-config
Building configuration...
Current configuration: 1072 bytes

<output omitted>

vrf definition red
vnet tag 3
<output omitted>

address-family ipv4
exit-address-family
<output omitted>

interface FastEthernet 1/0/0
vnet trunk
ip address 10.1.1.1 255.255.255.0
```

What is the interface ID and the IP address of the subinterface created to host the virtual network named red? (Select two.)

A. FastEthernet1/0/0.3
B. FastEthernet0/0/0.red
C. FastEthernet0/0/3
D. 10.1.1.3
E. 10.1.1.1
F. 10.0.0.3

QUESTION 83

You are planning the configuration of Easy Virtual Networking (EVN).

Which of the given statements is accurate of an interface that will be an EVN trunk?

A. It needs to support 802.1q encapsulation
B. The interface can also be configured for VRF-Lite
C. The interface will support OSPFv3
D. The interface can support RIP

QUESTION 84

After an associate configured a DMVPN hub, you execute the given command on the hub router:

```
Router#show ip nhrp detail
10.1.1.2/8 via 10.2.1.2, Tunnel1 created 00:00:12, expire 01:59:47
Type: dynamic, Flags: authoritative unique nat registered used
NBMA address: 10.12.1.2
```

Which of the given statements is accurate of this output?

A. The NMBA address was statically configured
B. The NHRP information did not come from the NHS
C. The mapping was created through an NHRP registration request
D. The device at 10.1.1.2 is behind a NAT router

QUESTION 85

inspect the given output of the show ip route command and the partial output of the show run command from the router R63:

```
R63#show ip route

10.2.0.0/16 is variably subnetted, 2 subnets, 2 masks

C          10.2.1.0/24 is directly connected, Serial0/0
L          10.2.1.1/32 is directly connected, Serial0/0
     10.0.0.0/24 is subnetted, 1 subnets
S          10.10.10.0 is directly connected, Tunnel0
     10.11.0.0/24 is subnetted, 1 subnets
S          10.11.11.0 is directly connected, Ethernet0/0
S     0.0.0.0/0 [1/0] via 172.21.114.65, Ethernet0/1


R63#show run
<output omitted>

interface Serial0/0
ip address 10.2.1.1 255.255.255.0
ip verify unicast source reachable via rx
```

What will the router do with a packet with a source address of 192.168.5.5/24 and a destination address of 10.11.11.20/ 24 that arrives on the Serial0/0 interface?

A. forward it out the Ethernet0/0 interface
B. forward it out the Tunnel0 interface
C. drop the packet
D. forward it out the Ethernet0/1 interface

QUESTION 86
An associate creates the given access list that she plans to apply to an interface on a router:

access-list 100 permit ip any any log

What type of traffic could cause this ACL to place a heavy load on the CPU of the router, and what command could be used to reduce the impact of the ACL? (Select two.)

A. traffic that is CEF switched
B. traffic that is process switched
C. traffic that is fast switched
D. ip access-list log-update threshold
E. ip access-list logging interval
F. logging rate limit

QUESTION 87

Earlier today you created and applied an access list designed to restrict remote access to the router R62 ONLY from the device at 2001:DB8:0:4:: 32. During testing, you discover that it is not having the desired effect.

You execute the show run command and see the given partial output that is relevant to the issue:

```
<output omitted>

ipv6 access-list secureaccess
permit ipv6 host 2001:DB8:0:4::32 any eq ssh

line vty 0 14

<output omitted>
FastEthernet0/0/1
ipv6 access-class secureaccess in
```

Why is the access list not functioning correctly?

A. the IPv6 address in the list is not formatted correctly
B. the list is not applied to the proper interface
C. the list is missing a deny statement
D. the ipv6 access-group command must be used to apply the list

QUESTION 88

Which of the given commands needs to be present in the configuration to support Unicast RFP?

A. bandwidth
B. ip cef
C. ip route 0.0.0.0 0.0.0.0
D. log

QUESTION 89

When the auth keyword is used in the snmp-server host command, which of the flowing needs to be configured with an verification mechanism?

A. the interface
B. the host
C. the user
D. the group

QUESTION 90

You in recent times performed SNMPv3 to increase the security of your network management system. A partial output of the show run command displays the given output that relates to SNMP.

<output omitted>

snmp-server group NORMAL v3 noauth read NORMAL write NORMAL

Which of the given statements is accurate of this configuration?

A. it provides encryption, but it does not provide verification
B. it provides neither verification nor encryption
C. it provides verification, but it does not provide encryption
D. it provides both verification and encryption

QUESTION 91

You execute the given command.

router(config-if)#ip helper-address 172.20.14.225

Which of the given traffic types will NOT be forwarded to the IP address 172.20.14.225?

A. TFTP
B. SMTP
C. DNS
D. TACACS

QUESTION 92

You have performed SNMP v3 in your network. You find after making the configuration changes that technicians in the RESTRICTED group cannot access the MIB. You execute the show run command and receive the given output that relates to SNMP:

```
<output omitted>

snmp-server group NORMAL v3 priv read NORMAL write NORMAL
snmp-server group RESTRICTED v3 priv read RESTRICTED access 99
snmp-server group TRAP v3 priv

!!
snmp-server user NORMAL NORMAL v3 auth sha CISCO priv des56 CISCO
snmp-server user RESTRICTED RESTRICTED v3 auth sha CISCO priv des56 CISCO
snmp-server user TRAP TRAP v3 auth sha CISCO priv des56 CISCO

snmp-server enable traps snmp linkup linkdown
snmp-server host 155.1.146.100 traps version 3 priv TRAP
```

What is preventing the RESTRICTED group from viewing the MIB?

A. the presence of the keyword priv in the command creating the RESTRICTED group
B. a mismatch among the verification mechanism and the encryption type in the command creating the RESTRICTED user
C. the absence of an access list defining the stations that can used by the RESTRICTED group
D. the presence of the keyword auth in the command creating the RESTRICTED user

QUESTION 93

Which of the given translation scenarios is NOT supported by stateless NAT64?

A. translation from IPv6 Internet to an IPv4 network
B. translation from IPv4 Internet to an IPv6 network
C. translation from IPv6 network to an IPv4 network
D. translation from IPv4 network to an IPv6 network

QUESTION 94

The given configuration is present on a router R1:

```
interface ethernet 0
     ip address 10.10.10.1 255.255.255.0
     ip nat inside

interface serial 0
     ip address 172.16.10.64 255.255.255.0
     ip nat outside

ip nat inside source list 7 serial0 overload

access-list 7 permit 10.10.10.0 0.0.0.31
access-list 7 permit 10.10.20.0 0.0.0.31
```

Which part of the configuration provides many-to-one access for all devices on the defined segments to share a single IP address upon exiting the external interface?

A. ip nat inside
B. ip nat outside
C. ip nat inside source list 7 serial0 overload
D. access-list 7 permit 10.10.10.0 0.0.0.31
E. access-list 7 permit 10.10.20.0 0.0.0.31

QUESTION 95

You have configured DHCP on a router and configured it to assign IP addresses in the range of 192.168.1.10 through 192.168.1.150. You just found that one of your print servers is using the address 192.168.1.100 and you cannot change it.

What command can you use on the router to solve this issue?

A. Router(config)# ip dhcp excluded-address
B. Router(config)# access-list
C. Router(dhcp-config)# ip dhcp excluded-address
D. Router(config)# dhcp exclude-address
E. Router(config)# service dhcp excluded-address

QUESTION 96

Which of the given translation mechanisms has the given features?
- Translates 1 to 1 Translates IPv6 to IPv6 Translates only the prefix
- Is deployed at the network edge

A. NAT64
B. NAT44
C. NPTv6
D. NPTv4

QUESTION 97

You have applied the given configuration to Router71, as indicated in the given partial output of the show run command:

```
<output omitted>

interface Ethernet0
ip address 171.16.6.5 255.255.255.0
no ip redirects
standby 1 ip 171.16.6.100
standby 1 priority 105
standby 1 preempt

<output omitted>

standby 1 track Serial0

<output omitted>

interface Serial0
ip address 171.16.2.5 255.255.255.0

<output omitted>
```

Which of the given statements is accurate of this configuration?

A. This is a GLBP configuration
B. 171.16.6.100 is the IP address of the HSRP group
C. The numeral 1 is the number of the HSRP group
D. This router will be prevented from taking back over as active router when it recovers from a loss of its Serial0 interface

QUESTION 98

You have been asked to troubleshoot the NTP configuration of a router named R70. After executing the show run command, you receive the given partial output of the command that shows the configuration relevant to NTP:

```
clock timezone PST -8
clock summer-time PDT recurring
ntp update-calendar
ntp server 192.168.13.57
ntp server 192.168.11.58
interface Ethernet 0/0
ntp broadcast
```

Based on this output, which of the given statements is accurate?

A. the time zone is set to 8 hours less than Pacific Standard time
B. the router will listen for NTP broadcasts on interface E0/0
C. the router will send NTP broadcasts on interface E0/0
D. the router will periodically update its software clock

QUESTION 99

Some of the technicians in your organization use the secure web interface to make some of the configurations changes on the router R68. Today it was reported that a technician could not make a connection to the secure web server. You execute a show run command on R68 and receive the given output:

```
<output omitted>
interface FastEthernet6
    no ip address
!
interface FastEthernet7
    no ip address
!
interface FastEthernet8
    no ip address
!
interface FastEthernet9
    switchport mode trunk
    no ip address
!
interface FastEthernet0
    ip address 192.1.12.2 255.255.255.0
    no ip directed-broadcast (default)
    ip nat outside
    ip access-group 103 in
    no cdp enable
    crypto ipsec client ezvpn ezvpnclient outside
    crypto map static-map
    duplex auto
    speed auto
!
interface FastEthernet1
    no ip address
    duplex auto
    speed auto
<output omitted>
ip classless
!
ip http server
ip http secure-server
ip http secure-port 1025
!
```

What needs to the technician do to make the connection to the secure web interface?

A. specify port 443 in the command
B. specify port 1025 in the command
C. disable the HTTP server first
D. enable the secure server

QUESTION 100

You just received the given system message.

```
*Mar 1 18:46:11:553 %SYS-5-CONFIG_I: Configured from console by vty2
(10.34.195.36) (Switch-2)
```

With this message in mind, which of the given commands were performed on the device? (Select all that apply.)

A. logging console level notifications
B. logging console level 4
C. service timestamps log datetime msec
D. service timestamps log datetime

QUESTION 101

Which of the given statements is NOT accurate of NPTv6?

A. is transport agnostic
B. translates the entire IPv6 address to another IPv6 address
C. is check sum neutral
D. translates only the IPv6 prefix

QUESTION 102

You are configuring NAT64 to allow communication among a host running IPv6 and a server running IPv4. The router R1 sits among the host and the server. The router's Fa0/2/7 interface is connected to the IPv6 host, and the Fa0/2/6 interface is connected to the IPv4 server.

The IPv6 host has an IPv6 address of 2001::a00:1/128 and the IPv4 server is at 10.0.0.1. Below is the relevant configuration on R1:

```
interface FastEthernet0/2/6
ip address 10.0.0.2 255.255.255.0
    nat64 enable
!
interface FastEthernet0/2/7
    no ip address
    ipv6 address 2001::A00:B/128
        nat64 enable

nat64 prefix stateful 3001::/96
nat64 v6v4 static 2001::A00:A 10.0.0.10
```

When the IPv4 server responds to the IPv6 host, what IPv6 address will be in the source address in the packet?

A. 2001::a001
B. 2001::A00:B
C. 3001::a00:1
D. 2001::A00:A

QUESTION 103

Your network team is assessing options available to translate IPv6 address to IPv4 addresses. You have focused your attention on the variants of NAT64. One of your necessitates is the conservation of IPv4 addresses.

Which of the given versions of NAT 64 helps to conserve IPv4 addresses?

A. stateless
B. manual
C. static
D. stateful

QUESTION 104

Your network team is assessing options available to translate IPv6 address to IPv4 addresses. In which of the

given scenarios is stateless NAT64 NOT supported as a solution?

A. translating from an IPv4 network to an IPv6 network
B. translating from an IPv6 network to an IPv4 network
C. translating from the IPv6 Internet to an IPv4 network
D. translating from an IPv6 network to the IPv4 Internet

QUESTION 105

You are executing IP SLA and could like to use it to measure hop-by-hop response time among a Cisco router

and any IP device on the network. Which of the given IP SLA operations could you use for this?

A. ICMP path echo operation
B. Internet Control Message Protocol Echo Operation
C. UDP Jitter Operation for VoIP
D. UDP Jitter Operation

QUESTION 106

You have performed the given IP SLA configuration, as presented in the given partial output of the show run command:

```
ip sla 1
dns cow.cisco.com name-server 10.52.128.30 ip sla schedule 1 start-time now
```

Which of the given statements is accurate of this configuration?

A. it will find the response time to resolve the DNS name cow.cisco.com
B. it will find the response time to connect to the DNS server at 10.52.128.30
C. it will start in one minute
D. it will gather data from one minute

QUESTION 107

inspect the output of the show ip flow export command:

```
Flow export v5 is enabled for main cache
      Exporting flows to 10.51.12.4 (9991) 10.1.97.50 (9111)
      Exporting using source IP address 10.1.97.17
      Version 5 flow records
      11 flows exported in 8 udp datagrams
      3 flows failed due to lack of export packet
      0 export packets were sent up to process level
      15 export packets were dropped due to no fib
      0 export packets were dropped due to adjacency issues
      0 export packets were dropped due to fragmentation failures
      0 export packets were dropped due to encapsulation fixup failures
      0 export packets were dropped enqueuing for the RP
      0 export packets were dropped due to IPC rate limiting
      61 export packets were dropped due to output drops
```

Which statement is accurate regarding the results?

A. 15 export packets were dropped because there was insufficient memory to create the export packet
B. 3 export packets were dropped because CEF was unable to switch or forward the packet to the process level
C. 61 packets were dropped because the send queue was full
D. 8 flows were exported

QUESTION 108

You need to configure a Cisco router to act as a DHCP server and provide the given services: Hand out IP
- addresses for subnet 10.10.0.0/16
- Set the domain name for the clients to "Cisco" Set the DNS server to 10.10.0.1
- Set the default gateway to 10.10.0.1
- Prevent IP address conflicts with 6 print servers that have consecutive permanently appointed addresses starting at 10.10.0.20.

Which of the given sets of commands will successfully accomplish this?

A. Router1(config)# service dhcp Router1(config)# ip dhcp pool IPPool
   Router1(dhcp-config)# network 10.10.0.0 255.255.0.0 Router1(dhcp-config)# domain-name Cisco
   Router1(dhcp-config)# dns-server 10.10.0.1
   Router1(dhcp-config)# default-router 10.10.0.1 Router1(dhcp-config)# exit
   Router1(config)# ip dhcp excluded-address 10.10.0.20 10.10.0.25

B. Router1(config)# service dhcp Router1(config)# dhcp pool IPPool
   Router1(dhcp-config)# network 10.10.0.0 255.255.0.0 Router1(dhcp-config)# domain-name Cisco
   Router1(dhcp-config)# dns-server 10.10.0.1
   Router1(dhcp-config)# default-router 10.10.0.1 Router1(dhcp-config)# exit
   Router1(config)# ip dhcp excluded-address 10.10.0.20 10.10.0.25

C. Router1(config)# service dhcp Router1(config)# ip dhcp pool IPPool
   Router1(dhcp-config)# network 10.10.0.0 255.255.0.0 Router1(dhcp-config)# domain-name Cisco
   Router1(dhcp-config)# dns-server 10.10.0.1

   Router1(dhcp-config)# default-gateway 10.10.0.1 Router1(dhcp-config)# exit
   Router1(config)# ip dhcp excluded-address 10.10.0.20 10.10.0.25

D. Router1(config)# service dhcp Router1(config)# ip dhcp pool IPPool
   Router1(dhcp-config)# network 10.10.0.0 255.255.0.0 Router1(dhcp-config)# domain-name Cisco
   Router1(dhcp-config)# dns-server 10.10.0.1
   Router1(dhcp-config)# default-router 10.10.0.1 Router1(dhcp-config)# exit
   Router1(config)# ip dhcp excluded-address 10.10.0.20 - 10.10.0.25

QUESTION 109

Your network team is assessing options available to translate IPv6 address to IPv4 addresses. Which of the

given is an advantage of NAT64 over NAT-PT as a translation option?

A. DNS64 and NAT64 functions are completely separated
B. DNS64 and NAT64 functions are completely integrated
C. NAT64 only works over an Ethernet network
D. NAT64 will be unable to reconstruct fragments packets if they are fragmented by an intermediate IPv4 router

QUESTION 110
You configured a device as an IP SLA responder using the given configuration:

```
ip sla 9
 tcp-connect 10.0.0.1 23 control disable
 frequency 30
 tos 128
 timeout 1000
 tag FLL-RO
ip sla schedule 9 start-time now
```

Which line indicates that the device is not a Cisco device?

A. frequency 30
B. timeout 1000
C. tcp-connect 10.0.0.1 23 control disable
D. tag FLL-RO

QUESTION 111

Which command is NOT mandatory for inclusion in a plan to execute IP Service Level Agreements (SLAs) to monitor IP connections and traffic?

A. ip sla
B. ip sla schedule
C. ip sla reset
D. icmp-echo

Cisco IOS IP SLAs Command Reference > icmp-echo through probe-packet priority > ip sla schedule Cisco > Cisco IOS IP SLAs Command Reference > icmp-echo

QUESTION 112

What could be a use case for the HSRP configuration below?

```
interface Loopback0
ip address 171.16.6.25

interface Ethernet0
ip address 171.16.6.6 255.255.255.0

no ip redirects
standby 1 ip 171.16.6.100

standby 1 preempt

standby 1 track Loopback0.

interface Serial1
ip address 171.16.7.6 255.255.255.0
```

A. used to switch the active role to the other router in the HSRP group during a maintenance window
B. used to prevent this router from ever relinquishing the active role
C. used to prevent this router from ever performing the active role
D. used to allow preemption over multiple peers

QUESTION 113

Your assistant is interested in gathering statistics about connection-oriented operations. Which of the given must be done to enhance the accuracy of the information gathered?

A. configure an IP SLA responder on the destination device
B. configure an IP SLA responder on the source device
C. schedule the operation on the destination device
D. add the verify-data command to the configuration of the operation

ANSWERS

1. **Correct Answer: C**

   Explanation/Reference:
   :
   The IPv4 address of the IPv6 router is 208.48.107.192. In an automatic 6-to-4 tunnel, IPv6 addresses have the 2002::/16 prefix. The 32-bit IPv4 address of the IPv6 router is then embedded into the IPv6 address. The 32 bits of the IPv4 address is embedded in the second and third quartet of the IPv6 address. The second and third quarters in the IPv6 address correspond to D030:6BC0. The conversion of these hexadecimal digits into decimal is given as follows:

Hexadecimal Digits (in pairs)	Binary Equivalent	Decimal Equivalent
D0	11010000	208
30	00110000	48
6B	01101011	107
C0	11000000	192

   The IPv6 router does not have 10.176.15.131 as its IPv4 address. The 10.176.15.131 address is the IPv4 equivalent of the second and third quarter (05B0:0F81) in the source IPv6 address.

   The other two IPv4 addresses are incorrect as they pertain to neither of the two IPv6 hosts. Objective: Network Principles Sub-Objective:
   Recognize proposed changes to the network

   References:
   Cisco IOS IPv6 Execution Guide > Executing Tunneling for IPv6

2. **Correct Answer: B**

   Explanation/Reference:
   :
   The correct answer is to use the tunnel mode ipv6ip 6to4 command to complete the configuration of an automatic 6-to-4 tunnel. This command requires the use of IPv6 unicast addresses that have the 2002::/16 prefix.

   The types of tunneling mechanisms supported by IPv6 are: Automatic 6-to-4 tunnel
   - ISATAP tunnel
   - Manually configured tunnel GRE tunnel

   Apart from using a tunneling mechanism, interoperability among IPv4 and IPv6 can be provided by using a dual-stack infrastructure or Network Address Translation-Protocol Translation (NAT-PT). A dual-stack infrastructure allows you to use both IPv4 and IPv6 addresses on the same router/host. NAT-PT is used to translate IPv4 addresses to IPv6 and vice versa.

   The tunnel mode ipv6ip command must not be used to complete the configuration because this command specifies IPv6 as the passenger protocol and creates a manually configured tunnel.

   The tunnel mode ipv6ip auto-tunnel command is not crucial to enable automatic 6-to-4 tunneling on the border routers. This command creates an automatic IPv4- compatible IPv6 tunnel among the routers.

   The tunnel mode ipv6ip isatap command must not be used because this command creates an ISATAP

tunnel. Objective:
Network Principles Sub-Objective:
Recognize proposed changes to the network

References:
Cisco IOS IPv6 Configuration Guide; Executing Tunneling for IPv6 > Configuring Manual IPv6 Tunnels
Cisco > Cisco IOS IPv6 Command Reference > tunnel mode ipv6ip

3. **Correct Answer: BC**

   Explanation/Reference:
   :
   The 2002:c0a8:4b01::1/64 and the 2002:c0a8:7d01::1/64 IPv6 addresses must be appointed to the Fa0/1 interfaces of rtrB and rtrC, respectively. Automatic 6-to-4 tunnels embed the IPv4 address of the tunnel interfaces into the second and third quartets of the IPv6 address that has the 2002::/16 prefix.

   To assign IPv6 addresses to the tunnel interfaces, perform the given steps:
   2. Convert the IPv4 address of the tunnel interface into binary.
   3. Convert the binary equivalent of the IPv4 address into hexadecimal (IPv6).
   4. Append the hexadecimal equivalent to the 2002::/16 prefix to form the IPv6 prefix of the tunnel interface.

   For the Fa0/1 interface of rtrB, its IPv4 address of 192.68.75.1 is equivalent to the IPv6 address c0a8:4b01. This address is then appended to the 2002::/16 prefix, resulting in 2002:c0a8:4b01::/48. The remaining host bits can be filled with zeros. Similarly, the IPv4 address of the Fa0/1 interface of rtrC is converted to the IPv6 address 2002:c0a8:7d01::/48.

   The 2002::c0a8:2d01/64 IPv6 address must not be appointed to the Fa0/1 interface of rtrA. The Fa0/1 interface of rtrA has the IPv4 address 192.168.45.1. The IPv6 equivalent of the IPv4 address, which is c0a8:2d01, must be embedded in the second and third quartets of the IPv6 address instead of the seventh and eighth quartets. IPv4 addresses are embedded into the last 32 bits for ISATAP tunnels.

   The 2002:c0a8:4b01::1/64 IPv6 addresses must not be appointed to the Fa0/1 interface of rtrA. This IPv6 address is the equivalent of the IPv4 address 192.168.75.1, which is the address of the Fa0/2 interface of rtrB and not rtrA. Therefore, this IPv6 address must be appointed to the Fa0/1 interface of rtrB.

   Objective:
   Network Principles Sub-Objective:
   Recognize proposed changes to the network

   References:
   Cisco Press > Articles > Cisco Certification > CCNP > CCNP Self-Study: Advanced IP Addressing
   Cisco Press > Articles > Network Technology > General Networking > Cisco Self-Study: Executing Cisco IPv6 Networks (IPV6)
   Cisco > Support > Technology Support > IP > IP Version 6 (IPV6) > Configure > Configuration Examples and Technotes > IPv6 Tunnel Through an IPv4 Network Cisco IOS IPv6 Execution Guide, Release 15.2M&T > Executing Tunneling for IPv6

4. **Correct Answer: BD**

   Explanation/Reference:
   :
   The IPv6 address of the tunnel source is ::172.168.111.65 and the IPv6 address of the tunnel destination is ::172.168.222.80. These two addresses are IPv4- compatible IPv6 addresses, which are addresses that contain the IPv4 addresses of the tunnel source and destination.

   In automatic IPv4-compatible IPv6 tunnel, the IPv4 addresses of the tunnel source and the tunnel destination are used to define their IPv6 addresses. The IPv4 addresses of the tunnel source/destination are embedded into the least significant 32 bits of an all-zero unicast IPv6 address. The resultant IPv6 address has zeros in the most significant 96 bits and the IPv4 address of the tunnel source/destination in the remaining 32 bits.

In this case, the source of an automatic IPv4-compatible IPv6 tunnel has the IPv6 address 0:0:0:0:0:0:172.168.111.65, abbreviated as ::2.168.111.65. You can also convert this address into pure hexadecimal format, which could be ACA8:6F41.

Any of the given three addresses could be used to identify the BGP neighbor at 172.168.11.65:

0:0:0:0:0:0:172.168.111.65
::172.168.111.65
::ACA8:6F41

Similarly, the tunnel destination has the IPv6 address 0:0:0:0:0:0:172.168.222.80 (abbreviated as ::172.168.222.80). The hexadecimal form of the IPv6 address of the tunnel destination is ::ACA8:DE50.

Any of the given three addresses could be used to identify the BGP neighbor at 172.168.222.80:

0:0:0:0:0:0:172.168.222.80
::172.168.222.80
::ACA8:DE50

The other two options state incorrect IPv6 addresses of the tunnel source and the tunnel destination. Both options specify an IPv6 address that has the IPv4 address of the tunnel source/destination in the most significant 32 bits and zeros in the least significant 96 bits.

Objective: Network Principles Sub-Objective:

Recognize proposed changes to the network

References:
Home > Support > Technology Support > IP > IP Version 6 (IPv6) > Configure > Configuration Examples and Technotes > IPv6 Tunnel Through an IPv4 Network > Configure > Configurations (Automatic IPv4-Compatible Mode)
Cisco IOS IPv6 Execution Guide > Executing Tunneling for IPv6
Cisco > Support > Technology Support > IP > IP Version 6 (IPv6) > Technology Information > Technology White Paper > IPv6 Deployment Strategies > Selecting a Deployment Strategy > Deploying IPv6 Over IPv4 Tunnels > Automatic IPv4-Compatible Tunnel

5. Correct Answer: AD

Explanation/Reference:
:
The given statements are ACCURATE about manually configured tunnels and GRE tunnels:
- Manually configured tunnels use the tunnel mode ipv6ip command, while GRE tunnels use the tunnel mode gre ip command. Manually configured tunnels do not support multiple passenger protocols, while GRE tunnels support them.

Manually configured tunnels and Generic Routing Encapsulation (GRE) tunnels are static point-to-point tunneling methods. Both of these tunneling methods provide a permanent link among two IPv6 networks that are separated by an IPv4 backbone. For each link among two IPv6 networks, a separate tunnel needs to be created.

Manually configured tunnels use a particular passenger protocol and do not support multiple passenger protocols at the same time. However, GRE tunnels can instantaneously use various passenger protocols.

It is incorrect to state that manually configured tunnels support IPv6 IGPs, while GRE tunnels do not. GRE tunnels also support IPv6 IGPs, such as OSPF, RIP, and IS-IS.

It is incorrect to state that manually configured tunnels block IPv6 multicasts, while GRE forwards them.

Manually configured tunnels also forward IPv6 multicasts. Objective:

Network Principles

Sub-Objective:
Recognize proposed changes to the network

References:
Cisco IOS IPv6 Configuration Guide, Release 12.4 > Executing Tunneling for IPv6 > Configuration Examples for Executing Tunneling for IPv6 > Example: Configuring Manual IPv6 Tunnels

6. **Correct Answer: B**

   Explanation/Reference:
   :
   When the routers in the network are capable of routing both IPv6 and IPv4 traffic, it is referred to as dual stack. The dual stack routers simply recognize the version a frame is using and react accordingly to each frame.

   Network Address Translation- Port Translation (NAT-PT) is a service that runs on a router or server that converts IPv4 traffic to IPv6, and vice versa. This eliminates the need for the routers or clients to be dual stack-capable. When only one router take places among the IPv4 and the IPv6 networks, this will be the only option, since all other methods listed require a dual stack capable device on each end of the tunnel. The IPv6 to IPv4 mapping can be obtained by the host from a DNS server, or the mapping can be statically defined on the NAT device.

   6to4 tunnels can be created among dual stack routers or among a dual stack router and a dual stack client. In either case, each tunnel endpoint will have both an IPv6 and an IPv4 address. When traffic needs to cross an area where IPv6 is not supported, the tunnel can be used to transport the IPv6 packet within an IPv4 frame. When the frame reaches the end of the tunnel, the IPv4 header is removed and the IPv6 frame is further routed based on its IPv6 address.

   Teredo is an alternate tunneling mechanism that encapsulates the IPv6 frame in an IPv4 UDP packet. It has the added benefit of traversing a NAT device that is converting private IP addresses to public IP addresses. 6to4 tunnels cannot traverse NAT devices by converting private IP addresses to public IP addresses.

   Objective:
   Network Principles Sub-Objective:
   Recognize proposed changes to the network

   References:
   Cisco > Home > Products and Services > Cisco IOS and NX-OS Software > Cisco IOS Technologies > IPV6 > Product Literature > White Papers > Federal Agencies and the Transition to IPv6
   Cisco > Cisco IOS IPv6 Configuration Guide, Release 15.2MT

7. **Correct Answer: BCE**

   Explanation/Reference:
   :
   When executing an automatic 6to4 tunnel, each IPv6 site receives a 48-bit prefix. The hexadecimal equivalent of the IPv4 address of the edge router is appended to 0x2002 and followed with the prefix to identify each end of the tunnel.

   Each end of the tunnel needs to be a dual stack router, which is one that can route both IPv4 and IPv6 traffic. For example, if the edge router's IPv4 address were 192.168.99.1, the hexadecimal equivalent of the address (c0a8:6301) could be inserted among 0X2002 and the /48 prefix, resulting in a packet with the IPv6 address 2002:c0a8:6301::/48 to arrive at the tunnel endpoint address.

   A Network Address Translation - Port Translation (NAT-PT) router performs translation from IPv4 to IPv6.

   It is not used in a 6to4 tunnel. Each site does not have a /16 prefix with a 6to4 tunnel. Rather, each site

   has a /48 prefix.

The IPv6 address of each IPv6 host is not part of the site prefix. These addresses are retained within the IPv6 portion of the header, and will be read after the frame reaches the end of the tunnel for eventual IPv6 routing on the far end.

Objective:
Network Principles Sub-Objective:
Recognize proposed changes to the network References:

Cisco > Products > Collateral > Whitepaper > Enterprise IPv6 Transition Strategy > IPv6 Deployment Solution Options

8. **Correct Answer: BD**

   Explanation/Reference:
   :
   If either the clear ip arp or the clear adjacency commands were issued, the entry could temporarily be listed as incomplete in the adjacency table. The adjacency table is used by Cisco Express Forwarding (CEF) to maintain Layer 2 information about the next hop to remote networks. In CEF, an adjacency refers to a control structure that holds Layer 2 information for an IP address on a particular interface. When that information is not available the entry will be listed as incomplete, as presented in the example.

   Layer 2 information normally comes from the ARP process. Therefore, if the ARP table is cleared with the clear ip arp command, the Layer 2 information will be temporarily unavailable until the ARP process re-learns it the next time a frame needs to be sent to that hop. Moreover, if the adjacency table is emptied with the clear adjacency command, the entry needs to be created again. This will also result in the entry being marked incomplete for a short period of time until the ARP table can be consulted and the Layer 2 information re-added.

   The interface in the scenario is not a multipoint interface. A multipoint interface could include entries for multiple next hops, since a multipoint interface connects to multiple Layer 3 destinations. An example of this is presented below in sample output from a Frame Relay interface:

   ```
   Protocol     Interface            Address
   IP           Serial0              140.108.1.1(25)
                                     0 packets, 0 bytes
                                     18410800
                                     FR-MAP      never
                                     Epoch: 1
   IP           Serial0              140.108.1.2(5)
                                     0 packets, 0 bytes
                                     18510800
                                     FR-MAP      never
                                     Epoch: 1
   ```

   The layer 3 information of the next hop is present in the entry in the scenario example. It is 10.10.10.2.

   Objective:
   Network Principles Sub-Objective:
   Identify Cisco Express Forwarding concepts

   References:
   Home > Support > Technology support > IP > IP switching > Troubleshoot and alerts > Troubleshooting Technotes > Troubleshooting Incomplete Adjacencies with CEF

9. **Correct Answer: C**

   Explanation/Reference:
   :

This behavior is called starvation and is caused by improper configuration of QoS queues. When TCP and UDP flows are appointed to the same QoS queue, they compete with one another. This is not a fair competition because the TCP packets will react to packet drops by throttling back TCP traffic, while UDP packets are oblivious to drops and will take up the slack created by the diminishing TCP traffic. The results from mixing UDP and TCP traffic in the same queue are:

- Starvation Latency
- Lower throughput

While it is accurate that jitter can be caused by a lack of QoS, jitter is not what is being defined in the scenario. Jitter is the variation in latency as measured in the variability over time of the packet latency across a network. This phenomenon seriously impacts time-sensitive traffic, such as VoIP, and can be prevented by placing this traffic in a high-priority QoS queue.

While latency can be caused by the maximum transmission unit (MTU) in the network, this is not a case of latency, although latency may be one of the perceived effects of starvation. Latency is the delay in reception of packets. The MTU is the largest packet size allowed to be transmitted, and an MTU that is set too large can result in latency.

While windowing can be caused by network congestion, this is not a case of windowing. This is a technique used to adjust the number of packets that can acknowledged at once by a receiving computer in a transmission. In times of congestion the window, or number of packets that can be acknowledged at a time, will be small. Later, when congestion goes down, the window size can be increased.

Objective:
Network Principles Sub-Objective:
Define UDP operations

References:
Design Guide > Service Provider Quality of Service > CE Guidelines for Collapsing Enterprise Classes > Mixing TCP with UDP

10. **Correct Answer: A**

    Explanation/Reference:
    :
    The correct answer is that IPv4 and IPv6 are running instantaneously on rtrA. The set of commands enables IPv6 on the rtrA router and assigns an IPv4 address and an IPv6 address to the Fa0/0 interface. This indicates that the router is a dual-stack router on which both IPv4 and IPv6 are running instantaneously.

    The IPv4 address is not translated to the IPv6 address by the given set of commands because NAT-PT is not enabled on the router. To enable NAT-PT on a router, you need to use the ipv6 nat command. In addition, the ipv6 nat prefix command must be used to specify an IPv6 prefix.

    The IPv6 address is not an IPv4-compatible address. IPv4-compatible IPv6 addresses are used in automatic IPv4-compatible IPv6 tunnels. These addresses refer to those IPv6 unicast addresses that have zeros in the first 96 bits and an IPv4 address in the last 32 bits. For example, 0:0:0:0:0:0:192.156.10.67 is an IPv4- compatible IPv6 address where 192.156.10.67 is an IPv4 address. The IPv6 address (2001:0:1:1:D52::F3C/64), in this case, is not an IPv4-compatible IPv6 address.

    A tunnel is not created for the interoperability of the IPv4 and IPv6 addresses because the given set of commands configures the router as a dual-stack router. There are no commands for configuring a tunnel on the router.

    Objective:
    Network Principles Sub-Objective:
    Recognize proposed changes to the network

    References:
    Cisco IOS IPv6 Configuration Guide, Release 12.4 > Executing IPv6 Addressing and Basic Connectivity > Configuration Examples for Executing IPv6 Addressing and Basic Connectivity > Example: Dual Protocol

Stacks Configuration

11. **Correct Answer: A**

    Explanation/Reference:
    :
    When an IPv6 packet is tunneled across a portion of the network that does not support IPv6, the IPv6 packet is encapsulated in an IPv4 packet using an IPv4 protocol type of 41. When it reaches the other end of the tunnel, the IPv4 portion is stripped off and the packet is routed the rest of the way by using the remaining IPv6 header.

    This method does not include a 20-byte IPv6 header with no options and an IPv4 payload. On the contrary, it includes a 20-byte IPv4 header with no options and an IPv6 payload.

    The maximum transmission unit is not increased by 20 octets with this method. Rather, it is decreased by 20 bytes due to the extra overhead.

    The IPv6 packet does not have its header removed and replaced with an IPv4 header. It encapsulates the

    entire IPv6 packet within an IPv4 header. Objective:
    Network Principles Sub-Objective:
    Recognize proposed changes to the network

    References:
    Cisco > Home > Support > Technology Support > IP > IP Version 6 > Configure > Configuration Examples and Technotes > Tunneling IPv6 through an IPv4 Network

12. **Correct Answer: BC**

    Explanation/Reference:
    :
    Tunnels and dual-stack are valid IPv4 to IPv6 migration strategies.

    Tunneling mechanisms can transport IPv6 across an IPv4 infrastructure. Cisco supports the given types of tunneling for this purpose:

    - Manual tunnels
    - Generic Routing Encapsulation (GRE) tunnels IPv4 compatible tunnels
    - 6-to-4 tunnels
    - Intra-Site Automatic Tunnel Addressing Protocol (ISATAP) tunnels

    For all tunneling types, IPv6 packets are encapsulated in IPv4 packets for delivery across the IPv4 infrastructure. These tunnels require two endpoints, either two routers, or a router and a host. Both endpoints needs to support IPV4 and IPv6.

    When executing an automatic 6-to-4 tunnel each IPv6 site receives a /48-bit prefix. The hexadecimal equivalent of the IPv4 address of the edge router is appended to 0x2002 and followed with the prefix to identify each end of the tunnel. Each end of the tunnel needs to be a dual stack router, that is, one that can route both IPv4 and IPv6. For example if the edge router's IPv4 address were 192.168.99.1, the hexadecimal equivalent of the address (c0a8:6301) could be inserted among 0X2002 and the /48 prefix, resulting in 2002:c0a8:6301:: /48 to arrive at the tunnel endpoint address.

    The given example shows a partial output of the show run command performed on a router hosting one end of a 6-to-4 tunnel:

```
router5# show run
!
interface loopback0
    ip address 64.101.64.1 255.255.255.0
!
interface Tunnel0
    ipv6 unnumbered Ethernet0/1
    tunnel source Loopback0
    tunnel source ipv6ip 6to4
!
interface Ethernet0/1
    ipv6 address 2002:4065:4001:1::/64 eui-64
!
ipv6 route 2002::/16 Tunnel0
```

The least significant 32 bits in the address referenced by the ipv6 route 2002::/16 Tunnel0 command correspond to the IPv4 address (64.101.64.1) appointed to the tunnel source. The hex equivalent is 4065:4001, yielding 2002:4065:4001::/48.

Another example of how IPv4 addresses can be used in the creation of the tunnel endpoint IPv6 identifier is presented in the partial output of the show run command performed on a router that is hosting one end of an automatic IPv4 compatible tunnel:

```
<output omitted>
interface Tunnel0
no ip address
no ip redirects
tunnel source Serial0/0
tunnel mode ipv6ip auto-tunnel
!
router bgp 100
no synchronization
no bgp default ipv4-unicast
bgp log-neighbor-changes
neighbor ::192.168.4.1 remote-as 100
no auto-summary
!
```

In the neighbor statement under the BGP configuration section, the neighbor address is derived from the IPv4 address of the other router (192.168.4.1). This could be performed in one of three ways:
- ::192.168.4.1
- 0:0:0:0:0:0:192.168.4.1
- ::c0a8:0401

The IPv6 addresses ::192.168.4.1 and 0:0:0:0:0:0:192.168.4.1 are performed by inserting the IP address at either the end of :: or 0:0:0:0:0:0. (:: is a IPv6 shortcut for 0:0:0:0:0:0). The IPv6 address::c0a8:0401 is performed by inserting the hex equivalent of 192.168.4.1 (c0a8:0401) in the same location.

Another potential migration strategy is to run dual stacks. The TCP/IP stack, or stack, is the TCP/IP software that is included in most operating systems. It is conceivable to run dual TCP/IP stacks on a computer. For example, servers and other infrastructure equipment often run both an IPv4 and IPv6 IP stack for application compatibility. This dual-stack configuration allows applications that require IPv6 to use the IPv6 stack and applications that require IPv4 to use the IPv4 stack. The given partial output of the show run command shows the configuration of a dual stack router:

```
<output omitted> ipv6 unicast routing

interface fastethernet0/0
```

```
        ip address 192.168.5.1 255.255.255.0
        ipv6 address 3ffe:b00:c19:2::3/127
```

This configuration allows applications on the same segment to communicate via IPv4 or IPv6. Dynamic

Host Configuration Protocol (DHCP) provides no benefits in migrating from IPv4 to IPv6.

IPv4 is not encapsulated in IPv6 in any of the migration strategies. IPv6 is encapsulated into IPv4.

Objective:
Network Principles Sub-Objective:
Recognize proposed changes to the network

References:
Cisco > Cisco IOS IPv6 Execution Guide, Release 12.4 > Executing Tunneling for IPv6

13. **Correct Answer: D**

    Explanation/Reference:
    :
    This behavior is caused by asymmetric routing. This is quite common in a routed network and usually is not an issue. It can, however, become an issue when firewalls reside in a routed path. Firewalls can cause issues when they maintain state information about connections. State information is used to define if return connection is allowed. If the return path is routed through a different firewall, it will not have the correct state information for the connection, and the return will be disallowed.

    It is not caused by windowing. This is a technique used to adjust the number of packets that can be acknowledged at once by a receiving computer in a transmission. In times of congestion, the window or number of packets that can be acknowledged at a time will be small. Later, when congestion goes down, the window size can be increased.

    The behavior is not caused by the maximum segment size (MSS). This value specifies the largest amount of data, in octets, that a computer or communications device can receive in a single TCP segment. This will not cause a packet to take a different path in the return than it did on its way to the destination.

    The behavior is not caused by worldwide synchronization. This take places when congestion on the network causes all devices to reduce their transmission rates at the same time. The result is the network cycling among sharp increases and sharp decreases in traffic.

    Objective:
    Network Principles Sub-Objective:
    Explain TCP operations

    References:
    Home > Services > Technical services newsletter > Tech insights > Chalk talk > Asymmetric Routing and Firewalls

14. **Correct Answer: D**

    Explanation/Reference:
    :
    The destination MAC address is the address of the BNG, so there is no need for it to be verified. If the traffic arrived on the BNG interface, it is correct.

    PPPoE is composed of two main phases, the Active Discovery Phase and the PPP Session Phase. The Active Discovery phase consists of the given communications among the PPPoE client and the BNG:
    2. The client sends a PPPoE Active Discovery Initiation (PADI) broadcast signal to the remote device (BNG).
    3. The remote device sends back a PPPoE Active Discovery Offer (PADO) that contains the MAC address of the BNG and destination MAC address of the subscriber (client).

4. The subscriber (client) send a PPPoE Active Discovery Request (PADR) continuing the destination MAC address of the BNG to which it wishes to establish a session.
5. The BNG responds with a PPPoE Active Discovery Session-Confirmation (PADS) containing the PPPoE session ID.

Once this process is complete, the session moves on to the PPP Session Phase in which Link Control Protocol (LCP) parameters such as maximum transmission unit (MTU) are agreed to, verification is performed, and Network Control Protocols (NCP) for any Layer 3 protocol that will traverse the link are started.
Objective:
Layer 2 Technologies Sub-Objective:
Configure and verify PPP References:

Cisco Support Community > ASR9000 BNG debugging PPPoE sessions
Cisco > Cisco Security Appliance Command Line Configuration Guide, Version 8.0 > Configuring the PPPoE Client > PPPoE Client Overview

15. Correct Answer: A

Explanation/Reference:
:
The method used needs to have been Password Verification Protocol (PAP). This method transmits the credentials in clear text, which makes it a poor choice.

There are only two methods available to authenticate a PPP connection, PAP and Challenge-Handshake Verification Protocol (CHAP). CHAP never sends the password across the link. Rather, the authenticating end of the connection sends random text and other information to the requester. The requester encrypts this data with its password and sends it back. The authenticating end of the connection reverses the encryption using the same password and compares the result with what was originally sent. If it matches, the authenticating end of the connection is assured that the requesting end knows the password.

The connection could not have used either 802.1x or IPsec, as neither method could transmit the credentials

in clear text. The connection could not have used CHAP. If it had, the credentials could not have been

captured with a sniffer.

Objective:
Layer 2 Technologies Sub-Objective:
Configure and verify PPP

References:
Cisco > Verification, Authorization, and Accounting Configuration Guide, Cisco IOS Release 15M&T > Configuring Verification > Non-AAA Verification Methods > Enabling CHAP or PAP Verification
Cisco > Verification, Authorization, and Accounting Configuration Guide, Cisco IOS Release 15M&T (PDF)

16. Correct Answer: B

Explanation/Reference:
:
The dead interval for OSPF will change to 40 seconds. By default, a Frame Relay connection that uses a physical interface is designated a non-broadcast network for purposes of determining the OSPF hello and dead intervals. There are four conceivable network types for Frame Relay, and they use different values for the OSPF hello and dead intervals. The values are presented below:

```
Network Type                Hello    Dead
Point-to-Point              10       40
Point-to-Multipoint         30       120
Broadcast                   10       40
Non-Broadcast               30       120
```

When the ip ospf network point-to-point command is performed, it will change the network type from the default of non-broadcast to point-to-point. This alteration will change the hello and dead intervals to 10 and 40 seconds, respectively.

The hello interval for OSPF will not change to 30 seconds. That is the value for non-broadcast and point-

to-multipoint networks. There will not be a designated router (DR) election. DRs are not elected on a

point-to-point network.

The hub router does not need to be configured with a router ID. In OSPF for IPv4, the router can create its own by using one of the IP addresses of its interfaces.

Objective:
Layer 2 Technologies Sub-Objective:
Explain Frame Relay

References:
Home > Support > Technology support > Initial Configurations for OSPF over Frame Relay Subinterfaces

17. **Correct Answer: B**

    Explanation/Reference:
    :
    The Broadband Network Gateway does not send a PPPoE Active Discovery Offer to the client during the PPP Session Phase. That action take places during the Active Discovery Phase.

    During the PPP Session Phase, the given steps take place: PPP options are negotiated.
    - Verification is performed.
    - Network Control Protocols (NCP) for any Layer 3 protocols that will traverse the link are started, and these Layer 3 packets will be transmitted within PPPoE headers.

    Objective:
    Layer 2 Technologies Sub-Objective:
    Configure and verify PPP

    References:
    Cisco Support Community > ASR9000 BNG debugging PPPoE sessions
    Cisco > Cisco Security Appliance Command Line Configuration Guide, Version 8.0 > Configuring the PPPoE Client > PPPoE Client Overview

18. **Correct Answer: CFG**

    Explanation/Reference:
    :
    In OSPF point-to-multipoint mode, the routers will automatically identify each neighbor. The election of a designated router (DR) and backup designated router (BDR) are not crucial. This RFC compliant mode of operation is commonly found in partial mesh topologies, such as hub-and-spoke designs. In the diagram presented in the scenario, router A is the hub.

    The frame relay serial interface has one DLCI to each spoke location. DLCI 221 is used by router A to communicate with router C and DLCI 222 is used to communicate with router B. On router A's serial interface, point-to-multipoint mode is enabled with the ip ospf network configuration command. The given is the syntax of the ip ospf network command:

    ip ospf network [{broadcast | nonbroadcast | point-to-multipoint | point-to-multipoint nonbroadcast}]

    The command parameters are as follows:

- broadcast - This mode enables the interface to emulate a LAN. This mode requires a full or partial mesh topology. nonbroadcast - This RFC 2328 compliant mode is also referred to as NBMA mode. The neighbors needs to be statically configured.
- point-to-multipoint - This RFC 2328 compliant mode is used in partial mesh topologies, such as hub-and-spoke. Routers use additional LSAs to discover neighboring routers instead of manually defining DRs and BDRs. The hub router floods link state updates (LSUs) by duplicating the update to be sent to each routers using the respective DLCI.
- point-to-multipoint nonbroadcast - This is a Cisco extension to the point-to-multipoint mode.

This mode is useful when the frame relay virtual circuits do not support broadcast traffic. Neighbors are manually defined.

There is no point-to-point parameter for the ip ospf command. Creating a point-to-point configuration differs in that the point-to-point parameter is performed as a parameter of the command that creates the subinterface that hosts the point-to-point connection as presented below:

Router(config)# interface serial 0.1 point-to-point

When configuring a serial interface without sub-interfaces, OSPF will check the encapsulation to define the network type. HDLC and PPP default to point-to- point while Frame-Relay encapsulation defaults to nonbroadcast.

The frame-relay map command identifies the mapping among the Layer 3 address (IP address) and the Layer 2 address (DLCI). The frame relay virtual circuits from the hub router are identified as supporting broadcast traffic by using the frame-relay map command with the broadcast keyword.

Objective:
Layer 2 Technologies Sub-Objective: Explain Frame Relay

References:

Cisco > Home > Support > Support Technology > Support > IP Routing > Configure > Configuration Examples and Technotes > Initial Configurations for OSPF over Frame Relay Subinterfaces
Cisco > Cisco IOS Wide-Area Networking Command Reference > frame-relay lapf n201 through fr-atm connect dlci > frame-relay map

19. **Correct Answer: C**

   Explanation/Reference:
   :
   The correct answer is show ip route ospf.

   The show ip route ospf command shows you all the OSPF learned routes in the routing table. An example of the command and its output are below with an of some of the terminology.

   Router5# show ip route ospf

   ```
   O IA 10.0.0.0/8 [110/65] via 5.0.0.2, 00:00:20, Serial1/1/0 S 0.0.0.0/0
   [110/1] via 5.0.0.2, 00:00:20, Serial1/1/0
   O E2 172.16.0.0 [110/25] via 5.0.0.2, 00:00:30, Serial1/1/0
   ```

- - indicates that the route was learned from OSPF.
- IA - indicates that the route is an inter area route, meaning it was learned via summary type 3 link
- state advertisements (LSAs). S - indicates that a static default route has been configured.
- E2 - indicates that the route is an external router redistributed from another protocol.
- Via - indicates the next hop address to use and the local interface from which to send
- [110/65]- indicates the administrative distance with the first value and the cost in the second (AD/cost).

The full legend of the conceivable route codes is below:

```
Codes: C - connected, S - static, R - RIP, M - mobile, B - BGP D - EIGRP, EX -
EIGRP external, O - OSPF, IA - OSPF inter area
```

```
N1 - OSPF NSSA external type 1, N2 - OSPF NSSA external type 2 E1 - OSPF
external type 1, E2 - OSPF external type 2
i - IS-IS, L1 - IS-IS level-1, L2 - IS-IS level-2, ia - IS-IS inter area
* - candidate default, U - per-user static route, o - ODR P - periodic
downloaded static route
```

The commands below can be used to monitor and verify OSPF operation:
    show ip route - displays known routes and from which protocol the routes were found, but for all routing protocols, not just OSPF.
    show ip ospf - displays the number of times the SPF algorithm has run and the default Link State Update (LSU) interval, but not the OSPF routes. show ip ospf database - displays the router ID, the OSPF process ID, and the contents of the topological database but not the routing table.
There is no show ip ospf route command.

Objective:
Layer 3 Technologies Sub-Objective:
Configure and verify OSPF operations

References:
Cisco > Cisco IOS IP Routing: Protocol-Independent Command Reference > show ip route

20. **Correct Answer: A**

Explanation/Reference:
:
The given command set will prevent the local router from advertising the 139.10.0.0 network out of the Ethernet 0/0 interface, while allowing all other networks to be advertised:

```
RouterA(config)# router rip RouterA(config-router)# network 10.0.0.0
RouterA(config-router)# network 139.10.0.0
RouterA(config-router)# network 199.10.10.0 RouterA(config-router)#
distribute-list 10 out e0/0
RouterA(config)# access-list 10 deny 139.10.0.0 0.0.255.255 RouterA(config)#
access-list 10 permit any
```

The distribute-list command allows you to apply a basic access list to a routing process. Just like applying an access list to an interface, when you apply it to a routing process, the permit statements define what networks may be advertised out the interface. The deny statements define what networks are not allowed to be advertised out the interface. Instead of applying the access list to an interface, you use the distribute-list command in router configuration mode to apply it to the particular routing process. By specifying an interface and a direction (in or out) in the distribute-list command, you can indicate where the advertisements will be blocked and in what direction.

Keep in mind that when applied this way, the access list does not affect what data traffic passes through the interface. It only affects what networks that the routing protocol will advertise. In the scenario here, RIP will not send advertisements for the 139.10.0.0 network out Ethernet 0/0, but traffic coming from or going to that network is still allowed through the interface in either direction unless there is an access list applied to the interface that will block it.

Conversely, if you applied an access-list to the interface that blocked traffic to or from the 139.10.0.0 network, but permitted all other traffic, it could not stop the routing updates about the 139.10.0.0 from passing through.

Note: The last command in the sequence, RouterA(config)#access-list 10 permit any, is VERY important. If that line is missing, any route not specified with an allow statement will be denied. For example, if you wanted to only allow one network to be advertised, you could configure an allow statement for that network and leave off the permit any parameter. It could block all advertisements with the exception of the one specified by the allow statement.

The given command set is incorrect because the distribute list is applied inbound, which could prevent the reception of updates concerning the 139.10.0.0/16 but could not prevent them from being advertised:

```
RouterA(config)# router rip RouterA(config-router)# network 10.0.0.0
RouterA(config-router)# network 139.10.0.0
RouterA(config-router)# network 199.10.10.0 RouterA(config-router)#
distribute-list 10 in e0/0
RouterA(config)# access-list 10 deny 139.10.0.0 0.0.255.255 RouterA(config)#
access-list 10 permit any
```

The given command set is incorrect because it applies an access list to the interface instead of a distribute list. The effect could be to block all traffic for that network, but allow routing updates:

```
RouterA(config)# router rip RouterA(config-router)# network 10.0.0.0
RouterA(config-router)# network 139.10.0.0
RouterA(config-router)# network 199.10.10.0 RouterA(config-router)# access-
group 10 out e0/0
RouterA(config)# access-list 10 deny 139.10.0.0 0.0.255.255 RouterA(config)#
access-list 10 permit any
```

The given command set is incorrect because it also applies an access list instead of a distribute list, this time incoming instead of outgoing:

```
RouterA(config)# router rip RouterA(config-router)# network 10.0.0.0
RouterA(config-router)# network 139.10.0.0
RouterA(config-router)# network 199.10.10.0
RouterA(config)# access-list 10 deny 139.10.0.0 0.0.255.255 RouterA(config)#
access-list 10 permit any  RouterA(config)# interface e0/0
RouterA(config-if)# access-group 10 out
```

Objective:
Layer 3 Technologies Sub-Objective:
Configure and verify filtering with any protocol References:

Cisco > Cisco IOS IP Configuration Guide, Release 12.2 > Configuring IP Routing Protocol-Independent Features > Filtering Routing Information Cisco > Cisco IOS IP Routing: Protocol-Independent Command Reference > distribute-list out (IP)

21. **Correct Answer: C**

Explanation/Reference:
:
The show ip eigrp topology all-links command displays both feasible successors and non-feasible successors to a given destination network. This command displays the contents of the topology table and shows all the routes available for a given destination network.

An example of partial output of the command is below:

```
R2# show ip eigrp topology- all-links
IP-EIGRP Topology Table for process 666

Codes: P - Passive, A - Active, U - Update, Q - Query, R - Reply,
r - Reply status

P 172.17.1.0/24, 1 successors, FD is 2169856
via Connected, Serial0
P 172.16.1.0/24, 1 successors, FD is 2195456
via 172.17.1.1 (2195456/281600), Serial0
P 172.19.1.0/24, 1 successors, FD is 2297856, tag is 1
via 172.17.1.1 (2297856/128256), Serial0
P 172.20.2.0/24, 1 successor, FD is 2469831
      Via 172.17.3.1 (2469831/2413698), Serial1
      Via 172.17.1.1 (2475369/2443698), Serial0
P 172.25.1.0/24, 1 successor, FD is 2496831
      Via 172.17.3.1 (2496831/2413468), Serial1
      Via 172.17.1.1 (2596481/2501649), Serial0
```

The 172.20.2.0/24 network has a feasible successor. This can be defined by looking at the values in the parenthesis next to each route. The second value after the / is the advertised distance from the successor. This value needs to be less than the value of the feasible distance for a route to be considered a feasible successor. There are two routes for 172.20.2.0/24. The first route listed, via 172.17.3.1, is the successor route. Its cost is 246983122, which matches the feasible distance (FD). The second route, via 172.17.1.1, has an advertised distance of 2443698 (the second value in the parentheses after the /). Because this value is less than the FD (2413698), it qualifies as a feasible successor.

The 172.25.1.0/24 network does not have a feasible successor. The second route listed via 172.17.1.1 has an advertised distance of 2501649, which is greater than the value of the FD, (2416381). Therefore, it is not a feasible successor.

You must not use the show ip route eigrp command. This command displays only the best metric routes (successors) to a given destination network. A route has the best metric if it has the least feasible distance, which refers to the sum of the metric from a given neighbor to a destination network and the metric to reach that neighbor.

You must not use the show ip eigrp topology command without the all-links parameter. This command displays only the feasible successors to a given destination network.

You must not use the show ip eigrp topology zero-successors command because this command lists

those routes that do not have a valid successor. Objective:
Layer 3 Technologies Sub-Objective:
Configure and verify policy-based routing

References:
Cisco IOS IP Routing: EIGRP Command Reference > show ip eigrp topology

22. **Correct Answer: C**

   Explanation/Reference:
   :
   The no auto-summary command must be run on Routers A, B, C and F. When discontinuous networks take place in the network, as in this one, the auto summarization feature will prevent proper routing. Auto summarization is enabled by default.

   Discontinuous networks are subnets of a classful parent network address not located in the same area of the network. Because Routers A, B, C and F will all advertise a 10.0.0.0/8 network Router D will not only think that the 10.0.0.0/8 network is on two different directions it will be unable to discern the individual subnets connected to each, leading to connectivity issues. Executing the no auto-summary command on those three routers will allow them to advertise subnets, clearing up the routing confusion created by auto summarization.

The ip summary-address eigrp 500 172.16.0.0.0 255.255.0.0 command must not be run on Router D. This will manually configure the same summarization that is already take placering automatically, and will not solve the issue.

The auto-summary command must not be run on Router D. This function is already being performed automatically and is the source of the routing issue. It must be disabled instead.

Objective:
Layer 3 Technologies Sub-Objective:
Configure and verify manual and autosummarization with any routing protocol

References:
Cisco > Support > Technology Support > IP > IP Routing > Technology Information > Technology Whitepaper > Enhanced Interior Gateway Routing Protocol > Document ID: 16406 > Summarization

23. **Correct Answer: D**

Explanation/Reference:
:

The show ip protocols command gives information about any dynamic routing protocol, including EIGRP. With respect to EIGRP, it will show the K values as a part of the output. A sample is presented below:

```
Routing Protocol is "eigrp 77"
Outgoing update filter list for all interfaces is not set Incoming update
filter list for all interfaces is not set Default networks flagged in outgoing
updates
Default networks accepted from incoming updates EIGRP metric weight
K1=1,K2=0,K3=1,K4=0,K5=0
EIGRP maximum, hopcount 100
<output omitted>
```

The debug ip eigrp command displays real-time information about EIGRP packets that are received and sent. It does not contain K values. A single line of this command output is presented below:

```
Router# debug ip eigrp
IP-EIGRP: Processing incoming UPDATE packet
IP-EIGRP: Ext 192.168.5.0 255.255.255.0 M 386560 - 256000 130560 SM 360960 -
256000 104960
<output omitted>
```

The debug eigrp packet command displays general debug information, but not K values. A sample of this command output is presented below:

```
Router# debug eigrp packet
EIGRP: Sending HELLO on Ethernet0/1 AS 109, Flags 0x0, Seq 0, Ack 0
EIGRP: Received UPDATE on Ethernet0/1 from 192.195.78.24, AS 109, Flags 0x1,
Seq 1, Ack 0
<output omitted>
```

The show ip eigrp traffic command displays packets received, as well as statistics on hello packets, updates, queries, and acknowledgments, but not K values. Partial output of this command is presented below:

```
Router# show ip eigrp traffic
IP-EIGRP Traffic Statistics for process 151 Hellos sent/received: 220/205
Updates sent/received: 7/29 Queries sent/received: 2/0 Replies sent/received:
0/2 Acks sent/received: 29/14
```

Objective:
Layer 3 Technologies Sub-Objective:
Define and optimize EIGRP metrics

References:
Cisco IOS Master Command List, Release 12.4T > sa ipsec through show ip route dhcp > show ip protocols

24. Correct Answer: B

Explanation/Reference:
:
The debug command uses a good deal of router CPU time, so you must not initiate this command on an already overloaded router. It often requires the router to do extensive examination of the packets, requiring heavy use of resources at times.

You could also possibly overload the router just with the debug command. If the router is overloaded to the point that it is no longer responding to your EXEC session, you may need to reload the router to stop the debug output.

These additional steps can help to verify proper route redistribution:
- On the router not performing the redistribution, use the show ip route command to see if the redistributed routes are displayed.
- On the router performing the redistribution, use the show ip protocol command to verify the redistribution configuration, and use the show ip route command that to verify the proper routes are there from each routing protocol.

The trace command is used to discover the route that packets take to their destination. The show ip route command displays the routing table.

The show ip protocols command displays information about each routing protocol running on the router.

References:
Cisco > Home > Support > Technology Support > Dial and Access > ISDN, CAS > Design > Design Technotes > Important Information on Debug Commands > Document ID: 10374
Cisco > Cisco IOS Debug Command Reference > Using Debug Commands

25. Correct Answer: AC

Explanation/Reference:
:
The given set of commands creates a static default route on RouterA and redistributes this route into the EIGRP corporation network. The ip route 0.0.0.0 0.0.0.0 S0/0 command performed in the worldwide configuration mode creates a static default route on the router. The ip route command allows you to specify a static route. The redistribute static metric 1000 1 255 1 1500 command then redistributes the static default route into the EIGRP autonomous system (AS) 200. This implies that

the EIGRP network identifies the default route as an external route, and traffic to all unknown destination subnets will be diverted to the default route.

Alternatively, default routes can be advertised into EIGRP networks by either of the given methods: Using
- the network 0.0.0.0 command on the router
- Using the ip summary-address eigrp 200 0.0.0.0 0.0.0.0 command on the router

A summary default route is not created on RouterA in the scenario. If the ip summary-address eigrp 200 0.0.0.0 0.0.0.0 command was used on RouterA, then a summary default route could be created. The summary default route points to the 0.0.0.0 network with the null0 interface as the next-hop interface. Summary default routes are helpful for providing remote networks with a default route.

The default route is advertised to the EIGRP network because the redistribute command was performed. This command is used to advertise the default route to the EIGRP network.

Objective:
Layer 3 Technologies Sub-Objective:
Configure and verify default routing

References:
Cisco > Support > Technology Support > IP > IP Routing > Design > Design TechNotes > Configuring a Gateway of Last Resort Using IP Commands
Cisco > Support > Technology Support > IP > IP Routing > Technology Information > Technology White Paper > Enhanced Interior Gateway Routing Protocol

26. **Correct Answer: B**

   Explanation/Reference:
   :
   The correct answer is show ip bgp summary.

   Although show ip bgp neighbors will show you the status of your connections to neighbors, only show ip bgp summary shows it to you in a concise, summarized format, with one neighbor listed per line. It displays both iBGP and eBGP neighbors and the number of prefixes that have been learned from the neighbor. Below is an example of the output of the show ip bgp summary command:

   ```
   Router6# show ip bgp summary
   BGP table version is 10, main routing table version 10
   <output omitted>
   Neighbor V AS MSGRcvd MSGSent Tv/Ver InQ OutQ Up/Down State/Rcd
   192.168.5.1 4 6006 78 79 10 0 0 05:20:06 2
   192.168.6.1 4 6007 77 80 10 0 0 00:00:20 Active
   192.168.7.1 4 6008 81 81 10 0 0 03:00:00 Idle
   ```

   The given information can be obtained from this output:
   - The BGP session to 192.168.5.1 is established. A number in the State column indicates that the session is established. This number indicates the number of prefixes received from the neighbor.
   - Router6 is attempting to establish a BGP peering session with the 192.168.6.1 neighbor. This is indicated by the keyword Active in the State column.

   Several show commands can be used to verify BGP configuration and operation: show ip bgp - displays
   - the contents of the BGP routing table
   - show ip bgp summary - displays the status of BGP connections in a summary format
   - show ip bgp neighbors - displays information about the TCP and BGP connections to neighbors

   Objective:
   Layer 3 Technologies Sub-Objective:
   Define, configure, and verify BGP peer relationships and verification

   References:
   Cisco IOS Master Command List, Release 12.4 > a through b > BGP > Commands: show ip through T > show ip bgp summary

27. **Correct Answer: C**

   Explanation/Reference:
   :
   The show ip eigrp topology all-links command displays both the feasible successors and the non-feasible successors. Feasible successors refer to backup routes to a particular destination network.

   Routers compute the metric/distance of every route they learn from their EIGRP neighbors. There can be multiple routes to the same destination network. The route with the least metric value to a specific destination network is selected as the best path, or successor, to that network. However, if the successor goes down, the router computes the next best loop-free path to the same destination network, which is called the feasible successor.

Feasible successors needs to have a reported (or advertised) distance that is less than the feasible distance, or current best metric. The routes that are neither successors nor feasible successors are called non-feasible successors. The feasible successors and the non-feasible successors can be viewed by running the show ip eigrp topology all-links command. Sample output is presented below:

```
R2# show ip eigrp topology- all-links
IP-EIGRP Topology Table for process 164

Codes: P - Passive, A - Active, U - Update, Q - Query, R - Reply,
r - Reply status

P 172.17.1.0/24, 1 successors, FD is 2169856
via Connected, Serial0
P 172.18.3.0/24, 1 successors, FD is 2169856
via Connected, Serial1
P 172.16.1.0/24, 1 successors, FD is 2195456
via 172.17.1.1 (2195456/281600), Serial0
P 172.19.1.0/24, 1 successors, FD is 2297856, tag is 1
via 172.17.1.1 (2297856/128256), Serial0
P 172.20.2.0/24, 1 successor, FD is 2469831
       Via 172.17.3.1 (2469831/2413698), Serial1
       Via 172.17.1.1 (2475369/2443698), Serial0
P 172.25.1.0/24, 1 successor, FD is 2496831
       Via 172.17.3.1 (2496831/2413468), Serial1
       Via 172.17.1.1 (2596481/2501649), Serial0
```

The router at 172.17.3.1 is directly connected to three networks: 172.25.1.0/24, 172.20.2.0/24, and 172.18.2.0/24. The second network, 172.20.2.0/24, is listed as the source of the successor routes to those networks. The connection to the last network, 172.18.2.0/4, can deduced by the fact that the local router uses the Serial1 interface to connect to the two networks that the router at 172.17.3.1 is a successor for. Therefore, that router needs to be directly connected to the network on the Serial1 interface of the local router.

Objective:
Layer 3 Technologies

Sub-Objective:
Configure and verify policy-based routing

References:
Cisco IOS IP Routing: EIGRP Command Reference > show ip eigrp topology

28. **Correct Answer: B**

Explanation/Reference:
:
By default, Type 5 link-state advertisements (LSAs) do not include directly connected networks. To alter this behavior, you needs to execute the redistribute connected command in OSPF configuration mode. This command instructs the router to include these local interfaces in its advertisements, as follows:

RTA10(config)# router ospf 1
RTA10(config-router)# redistribute connected

You must not execute the command set that includes the redistribute static command. This instructs the router to advertise any statically defined routes that have

been configured, instead of those that are local to the router.

You must not execute the command set that includes RTA10(config)# redistribute connected. The redistribute connected command is presented being performed at the wrong command prompt, and will generate an error message. It needs to be performed in the OSPF configuration mode and not worldwide configuration mode.

You must not execute the given command set:

RTA10(config)# router ospf 1
RTA10(config-router)# network 192.168.5.0 0.0.0.0 area 1
RTA10(config-router)# network 192.168.6.0 0.0.0.0 area 1

The network commands will cause the networks to receive updates from the router, but do not allow them

to be advertised in Type 5 LSAs. Objective:
Layer 3 Technologies Sub-Objective:
Configure and verify redistribution among any routing protocols or routing sources

References:
Cisco > Home > Support > Technology Support > IP > IP Routing > Design > Design Technotes > Redistributing Connected Networks into OSPF

29. **Correct Answer: AC**

   Explanation/Reference:
   :
   The autonomous system number (ASN) of rtrA and the best paths among rtrA and the 172.161.81.7 neighbor cannot be defined from the given output.

   The show ip bgp neighbors command displays the TCP and BGP connections from a given router to its neighbors. This command is performed in EXEC mode. You can use various optional keywords to view different aspects of the neighbors. For example, this command can display the details about a given neighbor, routes advertised to or received from neighbors, and the prefix-list received by neighbors.

   In this case, the command is used to show the details about a specific neighbor of rtrA. The IP address (172.161.81.7) of the neighbor is provided in the command.

   The text BGP neighbor is 172.161.81.7 indicates the IP address of the neighbor. The text remote AS 151 indicates that the neighbor is in the ASN 151. It can also be defined from the text external link that the neighbor is an eBGP neighbor. For iBGP neighbors, the text internal link will appear. The router ID (RID) of the neighbor can be defined from the text remote router ID 10.8.22.4.

   The output also provides details about the state of the BGP connection, which is Established in this case. Furthermore, the duration for which the connection has been established, the duration for which BGP maintains neighbor relationship in the absence of messages, and the keepalive duration are also displayed.

   The state of the connection among the local router (rtrA) and the given neighbor (172.161.81.7) can be
- any of the given: Idle Indicates that the local router does not accept any connection from its neighbor
- Idle (admin) Indicates that the connection among the two routers has been shut down administratively by using the neighbor shutdown command Connect Indicates that the local router has already sent an connection request to its neighbor
- Active Indicates that the local router is listening for connection requests from the neighbor OpenSent Indicates that the local router has sent an OPEN message to its neighbor
- OpenConfirm Indicates that the local router has received a KEEPALIVE or UPDATE message from its neighbor Established Indicates that a BGP connection has been successfully created among the local router and its neighbor

The status of the connection among two BGP neighbors can also be viewed by using the show ip bgp summary command, as presented below:

```
rtrA# show ip bgp summary
BGP router identifier 10.1.1.1, local AS number 210
BGP table version is 45, main routing table version 45
!
!
Neighbor   V  AS  MsgRcvd MsgSent TblVer InQ OutQ Up/Down   State/PfxRcd
45.1.1.5   4  950  78   80   45   0   0   01:53:41  IDLE(ADMIN)
10.2.1.1   4  950  23   22   45   0   0   00:10:32  IDLE
10.4.1.1   4  950  12   56   45   0   0   00:56:06  ESTAB
```

In the above output, it can be defined that the command router bgp 210 was performed on rtrA because the local AS is 210 in the output. It can be defined that the command neighbor 45.1.1.5 shutdown was issued on rtrA because the state of the neighbor relationship with the router at 45.1.1.5 is listed as IDLE (ADMIN).

All the other options are incorrect because the respective details are displayed by the show ip bgp

neighbors command. Objective:
Layer 3 Technologies Sub-Objective:
Configure and verify eBGP (IPv4 and IPv6 address families)

References:
Cisco IOS IP Routing: BGP Command Reference > show ip bgp neighbors
Cisco > Cisco IOS IP Routing: BGP Command Reference > show ip bgp summary

30. Correct Answer: B

Explanation/Reference:
:
At the area border router (ABR), router R2, the no-summary keyword is crucial with the area stub command to create a totally stubby area. All other routers in area 5 will require the stub command without the no summary keyword. The given commands are crucial to configure R2:

```
R2(config)# router ospf 5
R2(config-router)# area 5 stub no-summary
R2(config-router)# network 172.31.200.0 0.0.7.255 area 5
```

R1 will require:

```
R1(config)# router ospf 5 R1(config-router)# area 5 stub
R1(config-router)# network 172.31.200.0 0.0.7.255 area 5
```

All routers within a stub area needs to be configured as stub, or adjacencies will not form. Besides the command to enable OSPF and the command to identify the area, the only other crucial command identifies the area as a stub. A totally stubby area does not accept any external network LSAs (Type 5) or any inter-area summary LSAs (Types 3 and 4) from entering the area.

Use the area stub command with the no-summary keyword to configure a totally stubby area. The diagram below shows the commands that must be performed on R1 and R2.

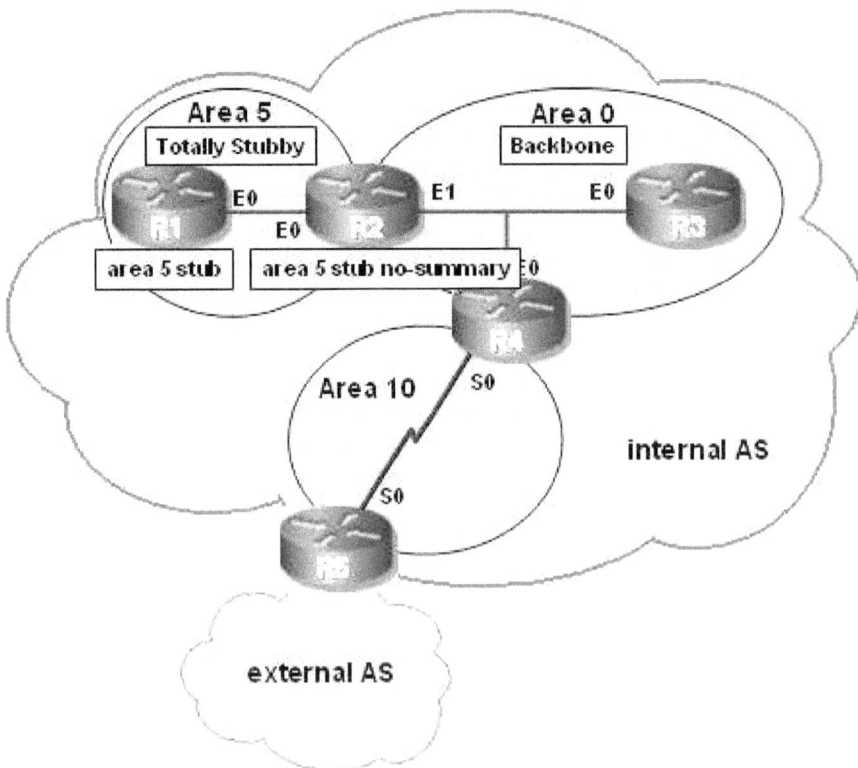

The correct syntax for the area stub command is presented below:

Router(config-router)# area area-id stub [no-summary]

Note that the optional no-summary keyword is used only on area border routers (ABRs) to block summary link advertisements into the stub area. This option creates a totally stubby area. It is very important to configure the command consistently on all routers within the area. OSPF sends its stub status (on or off) in its hello packets. If two neighbors have conflicting stub status, they will not form an adjacency, and you end up with no OSPF communication over that link.

Objective:
Layer 3 Technologies Sub-Objective:
Configure and verify network types, area types, and router types References:

Cisco > Home > Support > Technology Support > IP Routing > Design > Design Technotes > What Are OSPF Areas and Virtual Links? > What Are Areas, Stub Areas, and Not-So-Stubby Areas?
Cisco > Cisco IOS IP Routing: OSPF Command Reference > area stub

31. **Correct Answer: C**

Explanation/Reference:
:
EIGRP update packets are sent as a multicast when a new route is found, and sent as a unicast to synchronize topology tables when a neighboring router initializes.

Whenever EIGRP only needs to communicate with a single neighbor, it sends a unicast to that neighbor instead of the standard multicast. In this case, it unicasts a packet to update a new EIGRP router on the network with the information that all other routers on that network already know.

Hellos for neighbor discovery and maintenance are always multicasts. ACKs are hellos without data, and

are always unicast.

Queries are always multicast.

Replies to queries are always unicast. Objective:
Layer 3 Technologies Sub-Objective:
Define EIGRP packet types

References:
Internetworking Technology Handbook > Enhanced Interior Gateway Routing Protocol (EIGRP) > EIGRP Packet Types

32. **Correct Answer: A**

    Explanation/Reference:
    :
    The configuration indicates all steps are complete except for worldwidely enabling IPv6 routing. If that had been done, the configuration output could have reflected it under the interface as follows:

    ```
    interface S0/0/1
    ipv6 address 2001:610:FFFF:1::1/64 ipv6 ospf 100 area 0
    ipv6 enable

    ipv6 router ospf 100 router-id 10.1.1.6
    ```

    Prior to configuring OSPFv3 on an interface, it needs to be enabled worldwidely. OSPFv3 is an OSPF version specific to IPv6. The given commands will worldwidely enable

    OSPF v3. It will then be reflected by the ipv6 enable statement under the interface when viewing the configuration as presented in the fourth line of the output above.

    ```
    Router5(config)# ipv6 unicast-routing Router5(config)# ipv6 ospf 100
    Router5(config-rtr)# router-id 10.1.1.6
    ```

    The issue is not the router ID. The configuration in the scenario does assign a router ID, as indicated by these lines:

    ```
    ipv6 router ospf 100 router-id 10.1.1.6
    ```

    The issue is not the IPv6 address. The configuration does assign an IPv6 address to the interface, as indicated by these lines:

    ```
    interface S0/0/1
    ipv6 address2001:610:FFFF:1::1/64
    ```

    OSPF area 0 is not the issue. The configuration does place the interface in OSPF area 0, as indicated by these lines:

    ```
    interface S0/0/1 ipv6 ospf 100 area 0
    ```

    Objective:
    Layer 3 Technologies Sub-Objective:
    Configure and verify OSPF for IPv6

    References:
    Cisco > Executing OSPF for IPv6 > How to Execute OSPF for IPv6

33. **Correct Answer: A**

    Explanation/Reference:
    :
    The correct command is show ip bgp.

    The BGP table lists all the paths that the BGP router has learned. Each destination network listed might have multiple conceivable paths listed. Given that the criteria are met for each destination network, BGP will select a path to put in the IP routing table.

The BGP table is in many ways analogous to EIGRP's topology table in that it lists many known paths, not just the best path. Below is an example partial output of the show ip bgp command:

```
Router5# show ip bgp

BGP table version is 5, local router ID is 20.0.33.34
Status codes: s suppressed, d damped, h history, * valid, > best, i - internal
Origin codes: i - IGP, e - EGP, ? - incomplete
   Network          Next Hop        Metric LocPrf Weight Path
*> 10.0.0.0         0.0.0.0         0             32768  ?
*  30.0.0.0         20.0.33.40      10            0      35 ?
*>                  0.0.0.0         0             32768  ?
*> 11.0.0.0         20.0.33.40      10            0      35 ?
*>                  0.0.0.0         0             32768  ?
*> 192.168.0.0/16   20.0.33.40      10            0      35 ?
```

The given facts can be defined from this output:
- All of the routes were redistributed into BGP from an IGP. In the status column (located to the left of the Network column and to right of the column where some lines have a > symbol) is a column that is either blank or has an i symbol. In this case, all of the columns are blank. If the status column is blank, then BGP learned the route from an external peer. If it has an i symbol, an iBGP neighbor advertised this path to the router. It was learned from an Interior Gateway Protocol (IGP) and was advertised as a result of executing a network statement on the neighbor under the router bgp context as presented below adding the
30.0.0.0 network under BGP 100.

R4(config)#router bgp 100
R4(config-router)#network 30.0.0.0

- Four routes will be installed in the routing table. These routes have both an * symbol and a > symbol.
- I in the status column. The * symbol indicates that the next hop is valid and the > symbol indicates that this is the best route.

The output is slightly different if you specify the network that you are interested in, as presented below in the show ip bgp 214.5.98.0 command output:

```
Router 41# show ip bgp 214.5.98.0
BGP routing table entry for 241.5.98.0/24, version 48
Paths: (2 available, best #1, table Default-IP-Routing-Table)
Not advertised to any peer
5760
192.168.1.1 (metric 886) from 192.168.1.1 (192.168.1.1)
Origin IGP, metric 1652, localpref 100, valid, internal, best
```

This output focuses solely on the route to the network 214.5.98.0 and provides the given pieces of information: The neighbor that sent this route is at 192.168.1.1
The AS of the network where 214.5.98.0 is located is 5760
The IGP metric to reach the neighbor that sent this route is 886, as presented by the text 192.168.1.1 (metric 886) The complete metric to 214.5.98.0 is 1652, as presented in the last line by Origin IGP, metric 1652

The commands show ip bgp table and show ip bgp topology are not valid Cisco commands. The show ip bgp summary command displays the status of BGP connections.

Objective:

Layer 3 Technologies Sub-Objective:
Explain BGP attributes and best-path selection

References:
Cisco IOS Master Command List, Release 12.4 > l through q > Cisco IOS IP Routing: BGP Command Reference > show ip bgp

34. Correct Answer: C

Explanation/Reference:
:
When routes are being redistributed from the core into the edge and from the edge into the core, the administrative distance (AD) associated with external routes must be modified. This lessens the possibility of sub-optimal routing when multiple routing protocols advertise different paths to the same network. The AD associated with the externally advertised routes must be higher than the internal IGP's AD. To change the AD for an entire routing protocol, use the distance command. An example and the command syntax are presented below:

```
router(config)#router rip router(config-router)#distance 125
```

The complete syntax of the distance command is:

distance weight [address mask [access-list-number | name]

The weight parameter is the AD, which can be a number from 10 to 255. Note that distances 0 through 9

are reserved for system use. To change only the AD for selected networks, use an access list with the

distance command as presented below:

```
router(config)# access-list 5 permit 10.0.0.0 255.0.0.0
router(config)# access-list 5 permit 11.0.0.0 255.0.0.0
router(config)# access-list 5 permit 12.0.0.0 255.0.0.0 router(config)# router rip
router(config-router)# distance 220 0.0.0.0 255.255.255.255 5
```

The 0.0.0.0 255.255.255.255 portion included with the distance command could hold an address/mask combination for a single address, but it is more common to use an access list.

Objective:
Layer 3 Technologies Sub-Objective:
Configure and verify redistribution among any routing protocols or routing sources

References:
Cisco > Cisco IOS IP Routing: Protocol-Independent Command Reference > distance (ip)
Cisco > Support > Technology Support > IP > IP Routing > Design > Design Technotes > What Is Administrative Distance? > Document ID: 26634

35. Correct Answer: D

Explanation/Reference:
:
The missing autonomous system number (ASN) in the AS_PATH parameter of Path3 must be 40 so that Path3 becomes the best path from A to B. BGP selects the best path by first selecting the first valid path among two routers. If other paths are available among the two routers, BGP compares values of various attributes to select the best available path. In this case, Path 2 is the current best path among routers A and B. The values of various parameters (listed in the table) are compared with Path1 and Path2.

While comparing Path1 and Path2, the weight, LOCAL_PREF, local originate source command, length of AS_PATH, and origin type are same. Therefore, these parameters are not useful in determining the best path. However, the MED value of Path2 is lower than that of Path1. As a result, Path2 is selected as the best path because BGP prefers the route with the lesser MED value.

BGP now compares the parameter values of Path 2 (the current best path) and Path3. The weight and LOCAL_PREF parameters are same for both routes. Path 2
and Path3 are both local routes originated by using the redistribute and the network commands, respectively. BGP prefers local routes learned by the network or redistribute commands over those that are learned by the aggregate-address command.

The AS_PATH parameter specifies the list of AS numbers that comprise the route. The best path must have the shortest value for the AS_PATH parameter. In this case, both Path2 and Path3 consist of three AS numbers and are originated by an IGP. Therefore, the AS_PATH and the origin type parameters are not helpful in determining the best path.

Finally, BGP compares the MED values of Path2 and Path3. The MED values are compared only when the first AS number in the AS_PATH is the same for both routes; that is, when both routes begin in the same AS. The first ASN in the AS_PATH parameter of Path2 is 40; therefore, the missing ASN for Path3 must be 40. This allows the comparison of MED values and the selection of Path3 as the best route as it has lower MED value.

All the other options are incorrect because a value other than 40 disables the comparison of the MED values among Path2 and Path3. If the MED value is not considered, then BGP defines whether Path3 is an iBGP or eBGP router. BGP selects an iBGP route instead of an eBGP route.

Objective:
Layer 3 Technologies Sub-Objective:
Explain BGP attributes and best-path selection

References:
Internetworking Technology Handbook > BGP > BGP attributes

36. **Correct Answer: BDF**

    Explanation/Reference:
    :
    The given commands must be included in the execution plan:

    neighbor 135.90.66.6 route-map set_weight in match ip-address 1
    set weight 100

    The neighbor 135.90.66.6 route-map set_weight in command specifies a route-map named set_weight for the incoming routing updates from 135.90.66.6 peer. The match ip-address 1 command specifies a criterion to match the IP address as specified in an access list. When the match criterion is met, the action specified in the set weight command is performed.

    The set weight 100 command sets the weight attribute, which is a Cisco-defined attribute, to 100. The weight attribute is the first to be checked when BGP selects the best path among eBGP routers. This attribute is local to the router on which it is set and cannot be advertised to other routers.

    The complete set of commands to achieve the desired results is as follows:

    access-list 1 permit 10.77.22.0 0.0.0.255
    router bgp 444
    neighbor 135.90.66.3 remote-as 111
    neighbor 135.90.66.1 remote-as 222
    neighbor 135.90.66.6 remote-as 333
    neighbor 135.90.66.6 route-map set_weight in route-map set_weight permit 10
    match ip-address 1
    set weight 100

    The set metric 100 command must not be included in the execution plan to achieve the desired results. This command sets the metric to 100; however, the necessitate is to use the first attribute to be checked, which is the weight attribute.

The neighbor 135.90.66.1 route-map set_weight out command must not be included in the execution plan. This command forms an eBGP neighbor relationship with rtr3. The command also uses a route map named set_weight to set the weight attribute for the routes sent by rtr1. However, the weight attribute is local to rtr1 and cannot be set for outbound routes.

The route-map set_weight deny 10 command must not be specified in the execution plan to achieve the desired results. This command creates a route map named set_weight. The deny keyword in this command indicates that if the match criterion is satisfied, then the set action is not performed. The permit keyword must be specified instead of the deny keyword to perform the set action when a match take places.

Objective:
Layer 3 Technologies Sub-Objective:

Identify suboptimal routing

References:
Cisco > Support > Technology Support > IP > IP Routing > Design > Design Technotes > BGP Case Studies > BGP Case Studies 1 > Route Maps Cisco > Support > Technology Support > IP > IP Routing > Design > Design Technotes > BGP Best Path Selection Algorithm
Cisco > Support > Technology Support > IP > IP Routing > Design > Design Technotes > BGP Case Studies > BGP Case Studies 2 > Weight Attribute

37. Correct Answer: B

Explanation/Reference:
:
The neighbor with the IP address 10.2.1.1 has an established connection with RouterA. This is because the State/PfxRcd value for this neighbor is a number, 15, which indicates the number of prefixes received by RouterA from the neighbor. The prefixes are exchanged among BGP neighbors through the update message, which can be transmitted only if an established connection take places among the neighbors. An established connection take places among two neighbors if the local router is in Open Confirm state and it receives a KEEPALIVE or an UPDATE message.

The connection among RouterA and the neighbor with the IP address 10.1.1.1 is not established. This is because the State/PfxRcd value for this neighbor is OPENSENT. In this state, RouterA sends an OPEN message to a neighbor to define the parameters for establishing a connection. The OPENSENT state take places before the connection is established.

The connection among RouterA and the neighbor with the IP address 10.3.1.1 is not established. This is because the State/PfxRcd value for this neighbor is IDLE. In this state, RouterA does not accept any incoming connections from the neighbor.

The connection among RouterA and the neighbor with the IP address 10.4.1.1 is not established. This is because the State/PfxRcd value for this neighbor is ACTIVE. In this state, RouterA is attempting to establish a BGP peering session but it is not yet complete.

The connection among RouterA and the neighbor with the IP address 10.5.1.1 is not established. This is because the State/PfxRcd value for this neighbor is OPENCONFIRM. In this state, RouterA waits for a KEEPALIVE or NOTIFICATION message from the neighbor.

Objective:
Layer 3 Technologies Sub-Objective:
Define, configure, and verify BGP peer relationships and verification

References:
Cisco IOS IP Routing: BGP Command Reference > show ip bgp summary

38. Correct Answer: ABCD

Explanation/Reference:
:
Despite the inclusion of the command aggregate-address 192.168.5.0 255.255.252.0, all subnets of the aggregate route will also be placed in the routing updates because of the omission of the summary-only keyword. Therefore, 192.168.5.4/29, 172.16.5.0/16, 192.168.6.0/24 and 192.168.7.0/24 will be present.

Had the given command been performed, the subnet addresses could not appear in the routing table of

the router at 172.16.5.2: Router5(config-router)# aggregate-address 192.168.5.0 255.255.252.0

summary-only

Therefore, both the aggregate address and all of the 192.168.0.0 subnets will be in the routing table.

The 172.16.5.0/24 network will be in the routing table of the router at 172.160.5.1 because it is directly

connected. Objective:
Layer 3 Technologies Sub-Objective:
Configure and verify manual and autosummarization with any routing protocol

References:
Cisco > Cisco IOS IP Routing: BGP Command Reference > aggregate-address

39. Correct Answer: D

Explanation/Reference:
:
The eigrp router-id command must be performed in router configuration mode to fix the issue. This command specifies a fixed router IPv4 address to the router. If this command is missing or incorrectly configured on the router, EIGRP for IPv6 will not run properly.

Another command that you must perform so that EIGRP for IPv6 runs on the routers is the no shutdown command. You must execute this command in interface configuration mode. The no shutdown command is necessary because all the interfaces with EIGRP for IPv6 enabled on them are in a shutdown state by default.

A sample configuration to execute EIGRP for IPv6 on a router is as follows:

```
rtrA(config)# ipv6 unicast-routing rtrA(config) # interface Fa0/1 rtrA(config-
if) # ipv6 enable rtrA(config-if) # ipv6 eigrp 355 rtrA(config-if)# no
shutdown

rtrA(config-if) # exit rtrA(config)# ipv6 router eigrp 355
rtrA(config-rtr)# eigrp router-id 1.1.1.1
```

The two options stating that the ipv6 address command must be performed on the routers are incorrect. EIGRP for IPv6 can be configured on router interfaces without explicitly specifying a worldwide unicast IPv6 address. If you specify the ipv6 enable command, as in this scenario, then the ipv6 address command is not crucial.

The option stating that the eigrp router-id command must be performed in interface configuration mode is incorrect. This command must be performed in router configuration mode instead of interface or worldwide configuration modes.

Objective:
Layer 3 Technologies Sub-Objective:
Identify IPv6 addressing and sub netting

References:
Cisco IPv6 Execution Guide, Release 15.2M&T > Executing EIGRP for IPv6 > How to Execute EIGRP for IPv6 > Enabling EIGRP for IPv6 on an Interface

40. Correct Answer: D

Explanation/Reference:

R2 can establish a full adjacency with the neighbor at 192.168.5.107 and the neighbor at 192.168.5.165. In a broadcast, multi-access network OSPF network, full adjacencies can only be established with a designated router (DR) or a backup designated router (BDR).

Objective:
Layer 3 Technologies Sub-Objective:
Configure and verify OSPF neighbor relationship and verification

References:
Home.Support > Technology Support > IP > IP Routing > Design > Design Technotes > What does the show ip ospf neighbors command reveal? Cisco > Cisco IOS IP Routing: OSPF Command Reference > show ip ospf neighbor

41. Correct Answer: A

Explanation/Reference:
:
The area virtual-link command must specify the area to be traversed and the ID of the router to which the router being configured will connect. Therefore, the

correct answer is:

RouterA(config-router)# area 2 virtual-link 165.165.10.12
RouterB(config-router)# area 2 virtual-link 165.165.20.15

A virtual link is used to make a virtual connection of an area border router (ABR) to the backbone. It is used in situations where an area does not physically border the backbone area. The virtual link provides logical connectivity of the area to the backbone. If the virtual link appears not to be functional, which could manifest itself in Router A not having all of Router B's networks in its routing table, the state of the link can be verified on Router A by executing the show ip ospf virtual-link command. An example is presented below. The state of the link as presented in line 1 of the output must be up.

```
RouterA# show ip ospf virtual-links Virtual Link to router 172.16.8.2 is up
Transit area 0.0.0.1, via interface Ethernet0, Cost of using 10 Transmit Delay
is 1 sec, State POINT_TO_POINT
Timer intervals configured, Hello 10, Dead 40, Wait 40, Retransmit 5 Hello due
in 0:00:08
Adjacency State FULL
```

The configuration below is incorrect because area 0 is referenced in the second line. It must reference area 2, the area being traversed.

RouterA(config-router)# area 2 virtual-link 165.165.10.12
RouterB(config-router)# area 0 virtual-link 165.165.20.15

The configuration below is incorrect because area 0 is referenced in the first line. It must reference area 2, the area being traversed.

RouterA(config-router)# area 0 virtual-link 165.165.20.15
RouterB(config-router)# area 2 virtual-link 165.165.10.12

The configuration below is incorrect because area 0 is referenced in both lines. Both must reference area 2, the area being traversed.

RouterA(config-router)# area 0 virtual-link 165.165.10.12
RouterB(config-router)# area 0 virtual-link 165.165.20.15

If the virtual link is incorrectly configured the given error will be generated:

```
*Dec 10 00:31.146: %OSPF-4-ERRRCV: Received invalid packet mismatch area ID,
from backbone area needs to be virtual link but not found from 165.165.10.5,
Serial 0
```

Objective:
Layer 3 Technologies Sub-Objective:
Configure and verify network types, area types, and router types

References:
Cisco > Home > Support > Technology Support > IP Routing > Design > Design Technotes > What Are OSPF Areas and Virtual Links?

42. **Correct Answer: AC**

    Explanation/Reference:
    :
    Router7 is an area border router (ABR) and a backbone router (BR). The output reveals the link state databases for two areas, area 0 and area 2. Only ABR routers will display multiple databases when you execute this command.

    If Router7 is an ABR, then it is also connected to the backbone and will be a backbone router.

    Router 7 is not an autonomous system boundary router (ASBR) because it only displays sections in the output for Type 1 and Type 2 link-state advertisements (LSAs). ASBRs will also have a section for Type 4 LSAs, which could have its own heading at the end of the output.

    Router7 is not an internal router. A router is either an internal router or an ABR and Router 7 is an ABR.

    Objective:
    Layer 3 Technologies Sub-Objective:
    Configure and verify OSPF neighbor relationship and verification

    References:
    Cisco > Cisco IOS IP Routing: OSPF Command Reference > show ip ospf database

43. **Correct Answer: D**

    Explanation/Reference:
    :
    The routes that will be present in Router R1 are 192.168.5.0 and 10.0.0.0. According to the output, only the route from EIGRP 55 will be redistributed to EIGRP 200. Therefore, the 10.0.0.0 network will be advertised to Router R1 from Router R2 and the 192.168.5.0 network, which is present in the routing table of Router R2, will be advertised to Router R1.

    The 192.168.5.0 network alone could not be correct. The 10.0.0.0 network will be present as well.

    The 172.50.0.0 network will not be present because Router 2 is not configured with a redistribution statement for that network. The crucial statement could be redistribute ospf 1.

    Objective:
    Layer 3 Technologies Sub-Objective:
    Configure and verify redistribution among any routing protocols or routing sources

    References:
    Cisco > Home > Support > Technology Support > IP > IP Version 6 > Configure > Configuration Examples and Technotes > Redistributing Routing Protocols

44. **Correct Answer: AE**

    Explanation/Reference:
    :
    The R3 and the R9 routers in the scenario generate network link advertisements (NLA). An NLA or a Type 2 LSA is generated only by the designated router (DR) of a segment. Type 2 LSAs are generated only for those networks in which a DR has been selected. A DR is a router that has the highest OSPF priority on a segment. Until there are two OSPF routers on the segment, no Type 2 LSAs will be generated.

    Type 2 LSAs are flooded in the area that contains the network segment with the DR. These advertisements are used by the DR to represent the routers that are connected to the network. This type of LSA is sent to those routers that belong to the same network as the DR. Therefore, in this case, Type 2 LSAs are generated by the R3 and the R9 routers. R3 sends the LSAs to R1, R2, and R4, while R9 sends LSAs to R8, R10, and R11.

    R4, R7, or R8 will not send NLAs or Type 2 LSAs. These three routers are area border routers (ABR) for different OSPF areas. Like any other OSPF router, these routers generate Type 1 LSAs or router link advertisements (RLA). The LSAs contain the state of the routers that belong to same area. In this case, R4 generates and floods Type 1 LSAs into Area 0 and Area 10. Similarly, R7 and R8 flood Type 1 LSAs into Area 0 and Area 20, and Area 0 and Area 30, respectively.

    ABRs also generate Type 3 and Type 4 LSAs or summary link advertisements (SLA). These LSAs are flooded into other areas to and from the backbone area. Type 3 LSAs contain the list of networks that are exchanged among two areas. In this case, R4 floods Type 3 LSAs into Area 0 and Area 10; R7 floods these LSAs into Area 0 and Area 20; and R8 floods them into Area 0 and Area 30. Type 4 LSAs list the routes that point to autonomous system boundary router (ASBR).

    R13 will not generate Type 2 LSAs. R13 is an Area System Border Router (ASBR), which generate Type 5 LSAs apart from Type 1 LSAs. Type 5 LSAs, or external link advertisements, list the routes external to the AS; they are flooded throughout the OSPF domain except for stub areas.

    Objective:
    Layer 3 Technologies Sub-Objective:
    Configure and verify network types, area types, and router types

    References:
    Cisco > Home > Support > Technology Support > IP > IP Routing > Technology Information > Technology Whitepaper > OSPF Design Guide

45. **Correct Answer: A**

    Explanation/Reference:
    :
    The issue is that the metric was not configured. Some routing protocols require that a metric be provided for the redistributed routing protocol or route redistribution will not take place successfully. RIP and EIGRP both require that a metric be provided. IS-IS and OSPF do not have this necessitate.

    When you redistribute traffic into EIGRP without specifying a metric, then the default metric applied is zero, the route will be treated as unreachable, and the route will not be advertised. The addition of the metric parameter as presented below could solve this issue:

    Router9(config)# router eigrp 100
    Router9(config-router)# redistribute ospf 20 metric 10000 100 255 1 1500

    In this example, 1000 is the bandwidth, 100 is the delay, 255 is the reliability, 1 is the load, and 1500 is

    the MTU. The process IDs are correct in the original scenario, and the command was performed in the

    correct context.

    Objective:

Layer 3 Technologies Sub-Objective:
Configure and verify redistribution among any routing protocols or routing sources

References:
Cisco > Home > Support > Technology Support > IP > IP Version 6 > Configure > Configuration Examples and Technotes > Redistributing Routing Protocols

46. Correct Answer: B
Explanation/Reference:
:
All routers within a stub area needs to be configured as stub, or adjacencies will not form. Besides the command to enable OSPF and the command to identify the area, the only other crucial command identifies the area as a stub. At the area border router (ABR), R2, the no-summary keyword is crucial. The given commands are crucial to configure R1:

R1(config)# router ospf 5 R1(config-router)# area 5 stub
R1(config-router)# network 192.168.5.0 0.0.0.255 area 5

A totally stubby area does not accept any external network LSAs (Type 5) or any inter-area summary LSAs (Types 3 and 4) from entering the area. Use the area stub command with the no-summary keyword on the ABR only to configure a totally stubby area.

The correct syntax for the area stub command is presented below:

Router(config-router)# area area-id stub [no-summary]

Note that the optional no-summary keyword is used only on ABRs to block summary link advertisements into the stub area. This option creates a totally stubby area. It is very important to configure the command consistently on all routers within the area. OSPF sends its stub status (on or off) in its hello packets.

If two neighbors have conflicting stub status, they will not form an adjacency, and you end up with no OSPF communication over that link.

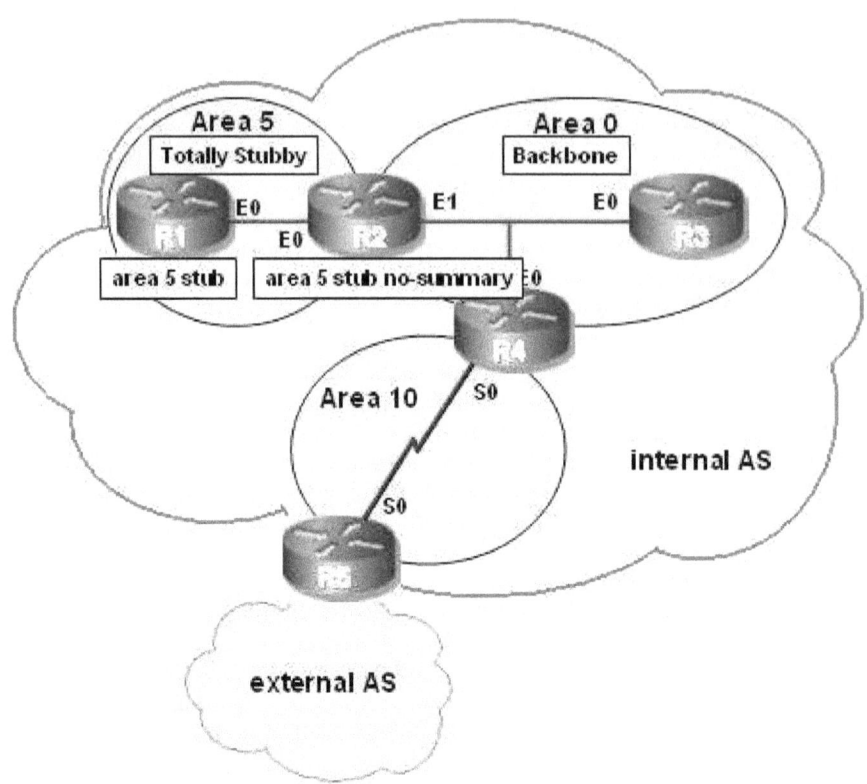

Objective:
Layer 3 Technologies Sub-Objective:
Configure and verify network types, area types, and router types

References:
Cisco > Home > Support > Technology Support > IP Routing > Design > Design Technotes > What Are OSPF Areas and Virtual Links? > What Are Areas, Stub Areas, and Not-So-Stubby Areas?
Cisco IOS Master Command List, Release 12.4 > a through b > area stub

47. Correct Answer: B

Explanation/Reference:
:
The only path is entered in the routing table as a result of the unequal load balancing configured on the

routers: RA-RB-RE-RI-RK

In EIGRP networks, bandwidth and delay are the default factors for calculating the metric/cost for a given route. Additional factors such as load and reliability can be considered in the computation of the EIGRP metric, as given in the given formula:

Metric = [K1 * bandwidth + (K2 * bandwidth) / (256 - load) + K3 * delay] * [K5 / (reliability + K4)]

In this case, only the K3 value has a non-zero value. This implies that only delay is taken into consideration to calculate the metric of the shortest path from
172.16.1.0 network to the WAN. The path with the lowest metric, which is delay in this scenario, is the shortest path, and is therefore entered automatically in the routing table. The total delay and the corresponding metric for the three best paths are given as follows:

```
Path              Total Delay    Scaled EIGRP Delay    Metric
RA-RB-RE-RI-RK         55               14080           14080
RA-RB-RD-RI-RK        100               25600           25600
RA-RC-RG-RJ-RK         70               17920           17920
```

In the given table, the path RA-RB-RE-RI-RK has the lowest metric of 14080. This is the shortest path, so it could be entered in the routing table even if variance were not enabled. In this scenario variance is set to 3, which enables unequal load balancing amongst those paths that have a metric less than three times the least metric for the given route. Three times the least metric in this scenario is 42240 (14080 x 3). This implies that paths among the 172.16.1.0 network and the WAN having a metric less than 42240 participate in the load balancing. On metric values alone, those paths could appear in the routing tables. However, to be eligible to be a feasible successor the reported distance of the path needs to be less than the feasible distance (current best path). None of the paths, with the exception of RA- RB-RE-RI-RK meet that necessitate.

The path RA-RB-RD-RH-RK is not entered in the routing table as a result of the unequal load balancing. The scaled EIGRP delay for this path is 43520 (170 x 256), which is more than three times the least metric available from the 172.16.1.0 network to the WAN (42240). In addition, the reported distance for this path is more than the feasible distance. Therefore, the path RA-RB-RD-RH-RK is not used for balancing the load from the 172.16.1.0 network to the WAN and does not appear in the routing tables.

Objective:
Layer 3 Technologies Sub-Objective:
Configure and verify EIGRP load balancing

References:
Cisco > Support > Technology Support > IP > IP Routing > Design > Design Technotes > How Does Unequal Cost Path Load Balancing (Variance) Work in IGRP and EIGRP? > Document ID: 13677

Cisco > Support > Technology Support > IP > IP Routing > Design > Design Technotes > How Does Load Balancing Work? > Document ID: 5212
Cisco > Support > Technology Support > IP > IP Routing > Technology Information > Technology Whitepaper > Enhanced Interior Gateway Routing Protocol > Document ID: 16406 > Feasible Distance, Reported Distance, and Feasible Successor

48. **Correct Answer: C**

   Explanation/Reference:
   :
   The correct answer is area 1 default-cost 25. Even though another option (area 1 default 25) is a configurable abbreviation for the command, the more correct answer explicitly specifies the default-cost parameter. The correct syntax for the area default-cost command is presented below:

   Router(config-router)# area area-id default-cost cost

   If you have multiple border routers among two areas, you might prefer one exit-point router over the other for that area. By configuring one with a lower cost than the other, it will become the preferred exit point. If that router or its links were to fail, then the routers interior to the area could route through the second-best exit point. You could also set the default costs to values that are close to achieve better load balancing. The default default-cost is 1. Please see the network presented in the graphic.

   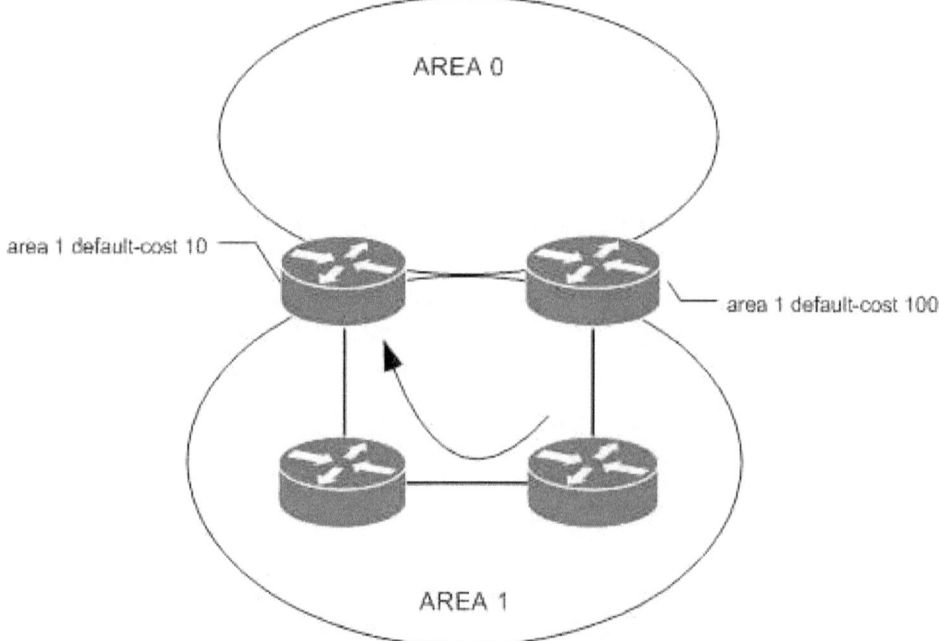

   All traffic will follow the path indicated by the curved arrow to the preferred ABR.

   Objective:
   Layer 3 Technologies Sub-Objective:
   Configure and verify OSPF path preference

   References:
   Cisco IOS Master Command List, Release 12.4 > a through b > area default-cost

49. Correct Answer: B

Explanation/Reference:
:
The FE80::260:3EFF:FE11:6770/10 address can be appointed to an interface of the IPv6-enabled router. This address is a link-local address as it has the prefix FE80::/10. Link-local addresses can be configured for an interface either automatically or manually.

Link-local addresses are IPv6 unicast addresses that are configured on the interfaces of an IPv6-enabled router. With link-local addresses, the nodes can connect to a network (local link) and communicate with other nodes. In addition, these addresses participate in the neighbor discovery protocol and the stateless auto- configuration process.

The FEC0:0:0:1::1/64 address must not be used for the interfaces because this address is a site-local address. Site-local addresses are IPv6 equivalent addresses to IPv4's private address classes. These addresses are available only within a site or an intranet, which typically is made of several network links.

You must not use the 2001:0410:0:1:0:0:0:1/64 and 2002:500E:2301:1:20D:BDFF:FE99:F559 addresses for the interfaces. These two addresses are worldwide unicast addresses as they fall in the range from 2000::/3 and to E000::/3. A worldwide address is used on links that connect organizations to the Internet service providers (ISPs).

Objective:
Layer 3 Technologies Sub-Objective:
Identify IPv6 addressing and subnetting

References:
Cisco > Understanding IPv6 Link Local Address

50. Correct Answer: A

Explanation/Reference:
:
The eigrp stub command is used to configure a router to send only connected and summary routes to its neighboring router. For example, examine the given output of the show ip route command that was performed on a router configured as a stub router:

```
router10#show ip route
C 172.16.5.0/24 is directly connected, Serial 0
D 192.168.7.0/24 [90/16523564] via 172.16.4.1, 00:21:20, Serial 1
D 172.16.0.0/16 is a summary, 00:21:23, Null 0 C 172.16.4.0/24 is directly
connected, Serial 2
```

The routes that will be advertised are 172.16.5.0/24, 172.16.4.0/24, and the summary route 172.16.0.0/16. The first two is directly connected routes, and the last is the summary route that is auto configured by the EIGRP process.

When the stub feature is enabled on a router, the router will announce itself as a stub router. Neighbor routers will not query a stub router for alternate routes when a route is lost elsewhere in the network. The EIGRP stub feature works well in hub-and-spoke topologies when the goal is to minimize the amount of EIGRP bandwidth and processing associated with the spoke router. The eigrp stub command has the given syntax:

eigrp stub [receive-only | connected | static | summary]

When you do not specify any keywords with the command, connected and summary are used by default.
- receive-only: Prevents the router from sending any connected or summary routes.
- connected: Instructs the router to send connected routes.
- static: Instructs the router to send static routes that were redistributed by using the redistribute static
- command. summary: Instructs the router to send summary routes.

These parameters can be combined to resolve various issues, as seen in the given image:

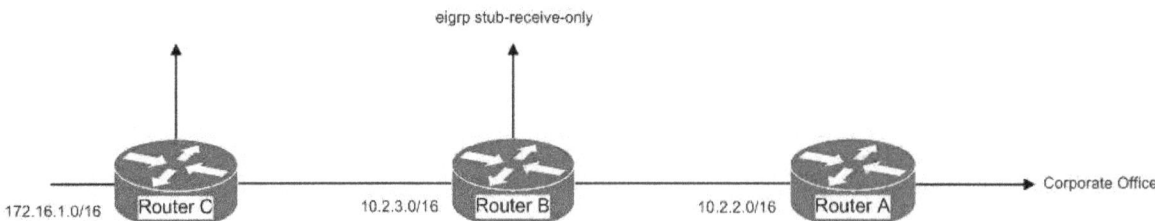

Router A is not receiving the route to the 172.16.1.0/16 network because Router B, which stands among Router A and C, is configured with the eigrp stub-receive- only command. This is resulting in hosts from the corporate office being unable to connect to hosts in the 172.16.0.0/16 network. If there were a legitimate reason to keep Router B configured with the eigrp stub-receive-only command, the issue could be solved by executing the given command set on Router A:

routerA(config)# router eigrp 20
routerA(config-router)# ip summary-address eigrp 20 172.16.0.0 255.255.0.0 routerA(config-router)# eigrp stub connected summary

This command set could create a summary address for the 172.16.0.0/16 network and then advertise it to the corporate office as a result of using the eigrp stub connected summary command. The inclusion of the connected parameter ensures that the directly connected networks will also be advertised, to ensure that hosts in the corporate office can reach the 172.16.0.0/16 network.

The eigrp stub static command instructs the router to send static routes that were redistributed by using the redistribute static command. inspect the EIGRP configuration presented below:

```
<output omitted>
ip route 10.4.4.0 255.255.255.0 10.4.3.10
Route eigrp 200 No auto-summary
Redistribute static 1000 1 255 1 1500
Network 10.4.1.0 0.0.0.3.
Network 10.4.2.0 0.0.0.255
Eigrp stub static
```

With this configuration, the router could not advertise any of the networks defined in the network statements, but could only advertise the static route configured with the line ip route 10.4.4.0 255.255.255.0 10.4.3.10.

Eigrp passive is not a valid Cisco command.

Eigrp stub receive-only will cause the router to not advertise any routes. The router will only receive updates.

Objective:
Layer 3 Technologies Sub-Objective:
Configure and verify EIGRP stubs

References:
Cisco IOS Master Command List, Release 12.4 > e through h > eigrp stub

51. Correct Answer: AC

Explanation/Reference:
:
EIGRP routers will not become neighbors if the K-values do not match or if the autonomous system (AS) numbers do not match. They also will not become neighbors if EIGRP is not enabled for the proper networks on the local and remote routers. However, routers can become neighbors if their hello intervals and hold times do not match.

The AS number is designed to control the routers with which a router can communicate. If the AS numbers do not match, EIGRP will not exchange routes among the two routers by design and definition.

The K-values are flags that state whether a certain metric component, such as Load, is used. They needs to match because they regulate how the metric values are calculated. If one router is just using bandwidth and delay to calculate its metric, and another is using bandwidth, delay, and load; they could make contradictory routing decisions that could lead to a routing loop. Because of this possibility, EIGRP requires that the K-values needs to match before it will allow the routers to exchange routes.

EIGRP does not require that the hello and hold times match. Although this flexibility can be helpful, it can also lead to unforeseen issues if they are accidentally mismatched. The hello interval is the amount of time in seconds to wait before sending another hello packet. The hold time is the amount of time in seconds to wait before declaring a link to be down.

Objective:
Layer 3 Technologies

Sub-Objective:
Configure and verify EIGRP neighbor relationship and verification

References:
Cisco > Home > Support > Technology Support > IP > IP Routing > Design > Design Technotes > Introduction to EIGRP > How does EIGRP work?

52. Correct Answer: A

Explanation/Reference:
:
The auto-summary command can affect which networks, identified by using the network command, will be advertised. Using the take placering BGP configuration, the router will not announce the 172.16.16.0/24 subnet. Instead, it will announce the classful address 172.16.0.0/16 when the IP routing table maintained by the IGP

contains any subnet of that classful address.

The network command directly affects what network is advertised in BGP. If the network command does not also include a network mask, and if auto-summary is enabled, the classful address of 172.16.0.0/16 is advertised any time that the router learns about a 172.16.0.0 subnet via its Interior Gateway Protocol (IGP), such as OSPF or EIGRP. In the display, the routing table does contain entries of the 172.16.16.0/24 and 172.16.24.0/24 subnets that were learned by using the IGP.

If auto-summary is disabled by using the no auto-summary command, only networks in the routing table that are exact matches to the network commands are advertised. For example, to have the router announce only the 172.16.16.0/24 subnet learned via its IGP, you must alter the network command's IP address and include the subnet mask as follows:

network 172.16.16.0 mask 255.255.255.0

A combination of network statements and route statements can be used to advertise a subset of networks that take place. inspect the output presented below:

router bgp 68410
network 192.168.24.0 255.255.252.0

neighbor 172.16.8.5 remote-as 68441
ip route 192.168.24.0 255.255.252.0 null 0

The router is configured to advertise a summary route to the network 192.168.24.0 255.255.252.0.

Consider the given networks: 192.168.24.0/24
192.168.25.0/24
192.168.26.0/24
192.168.32.0/24

If this router was connected to those networks, and received a packet destined for 192.168.25.1, it could successfully route the packet because the summary address (where the summarization is the result of the mask 255.255.252.0) is designed to include all of the subnets above except for 192.168.32.0/24. Therefore, all subnets except 192.168.32.0/24 will be advertised by the network and ip route statements with the summary mask.

Note: Whenever changes are made to a routing policy or to an access list that is used by a routing policy, the change will not be reflected in the routing tables of the receiving routers until the BGP session has been cleared with the clear ip bgp command.

The BGP synchronization rule specifies that networks will not be advertised or used via iBGP unless it also has been learned through an IGP. If synchronization is disabled, iBGP will advertise a network without also learning it through an IGP.

Objective:
Layer 3 Technologies Sub-Objective:
Configure and verify eBGP (IPv4 and IPv6 address families) References:

Cisco IOS Master Command List > a through b > BGP Commands: A through B > auto-summary (BGP)
Cisco > Cisco IOS IP Routing: BGP Command Reference > router bgp
Cisco > Cisco IOS IP Routing: BGP Command Reference > network (BGP and multiprotocol BGP)

53. **Correct Answer: C**

    Explanation/Reference:
    :
    The given command pair must be used to configure successful verification:

    neighbor 192.168.5.2 password routera performed on RouterA neighbor 192.168.5.3 password routera performed on RouterB

    When setting the keys for verification, the keys needs to match. The keys do not need to be the names of either router, and must be a combination of letters numbers and symbols. In this example, both keys are set to the value routera.

    The given two command pairs are incorrect because the keys do not match:

    neighbor 192.168.5.2 password routera performed on RouterA neighbor 192.168.5.3 password routerb performed on RouterB

    and

    neighbor 192.168.5.2 password routerb performed on RouterA neighbor 192.168.5.3 password routera performed on RouterB

    If you performed the debug ip bgp command to perform troubleshooting with either of these configurations in place, the error message you could see could be as follows:

    ```
    %TCP-6-BADAUTH: Invalid MD5 digest from 192.168.5.3 (12293) to 192.168.5.2
    (179)
    ```

In the error message, the numbers in parentheses are the port numbers used for the attempted

communication. The single commands could be incorrect because the key has only been configured on

one end:

neighbor 192.168.5.2 password routera performed on RouterA and

neighbor 192.168.5.2 password routerb performed on RouterB

If you performed the debug ip bgp command to troubleshoot with either of these configurations in place, you could see the given message:

```
%TCP-6-BADAUTH: No MD5 digest from 192.168.5.3 (12293) to 192.168.5.2 (179)
```

Objective:
Layer 3 Technologies Sub-Objective:
Define, configure, and verify BGP peer relationships and verification

References:
Cisco IOS Master Command List, Release 12.4 > l through q > Cisco IOS IP Routing: BGP Command Reference > neighbor password

54. **Correct Answer: D**

    Explanation/Reference:
    :
    The given command pair must be used to configure successful verification:

    neighbor 192.168.5.2 password routera performed on RouterA neighbor 192.168.5.3 password routera performed on RouterB

    When setting the keys for verification, the keys needs to match. The keys do not need to be the names of either router, and must be a combination of letters numbers and symbols. In this example, both keys are set to the value routera.

    The given two command pairs are incorrect because the keys do not match:

    neighbor 192.168.5.2 password routera performed on RouterA neighbor 192.168.5.3 password routerb performed on RouterB

    and

    neighbor 192.168.5.2 password routerb performed on RouterA neighbor 192.168.5.3 password routera performed on RouterB

    If you performed the debug ip bgp command to perform troubleshooting with either of these configurations in place, the error message you could see could be as follows:

    ```
    %TCP-6-BADAUTH: Invalid MD5 digest from 192.168.5.3 (12293) to 192.168.5.2 (179)
    ```

    In the error message, the numbers in parentheses are the port numbers used for the attempted

    communication. The single commands could be incorrect because the key has only been configured on

    one end:

    neighbor 192.168.5.2 password routera performed on RouterA and neighbor 192.168.5.2 password routerb performed on RouterB

If you performed the debug ip bgp command to troubleshoot with either of these configurations in place, you could see the given message:

```
%TCP-6-BADAUTH: No MD5 digest from 192.168.5.3 (12293) to 192.168.5.2 (179)
```

Objective:
Layer 3 Technologies Sub-Objective:
Define, configure, and verify BGP peer relationships and verification

References:
Cisco IOS Master Command List, Release 12.4 > l through q > Cisco IOS IP Routing: BGP Command Reference > neighbor password

55. Correct Answer: BD

Explanation/Reference:
:
Distribute lists are used to filter inbound, outbound, or redistributed routing updates. Instead of using the passive-interface command, distribute lists enable you to selectively control which routes are processed.

If no distribute list is associated with the interface, the routing update packets are processed normally.

If a distribute list is associated with an interface, the routing update is compared to the access list that was specified in the distribute list. If a match is found to a permit statement, then the packet is forwarded. If a match is found to a deny statement, the packet is discarded. If no match is found, the implicit deny statement at the end of the access list will drop the packet.

Network security is not the primary role of route filtering. Its primary function is to reduce unnecessary

routing update traffic. Route filtering on an interface can filter routes that originate from the same router.

The network keyword of the passive-interface command does not enable you identify the routes to advertise.

Objective:
Layer 3 Technologies Sub-Objective:
Configure and verify filtering with any protocol

References:
Cisco > Home > Support > Technology Support > IP Routing > Design > Design Technotes > Filtering Routing Updates on Distance Vector IP Routing Protocols Cisco > Cisco IOS IP Configuration Guide: Configuring IP Routing Protocol-Independent Features > Filtering Routing Information

56. Correct Answer: A

Explanation/Reference:
:
The EIGRP default hello time over a LAN or high-speed dedicated WAN link is five seconds.

On multipoint circuits with less than T1 bandwidth, EIGRP hello packets are sent every 60 seconds. EIGRP sets the default hello interval to five seconds to ensure that it can quickly sense if connectivity to a neighboring router has been cut. If a router does not hear from a neighboring EIGRP router in 15 seconds, it will declare that neighbor as no longer reachable.

The five-second hello interval is shorter than the default values for OSPF hellos (10 seconds), RIP updates (30), or IGRP updates (90). As a result, EIGRP senses network faults faster by default than do other protocols.

Objective:

Layer 3 Technologies Sub-Objective:
Configure and verify EIGRP neighbor relationship and verification

References:
Internetworking Technology Handbook > Enhanced Interior Gateway Routing Protocol (EIGRP) > Underlying Processes and Technologies

57. Correct Answer: A

Explanation/Reference:
:

The ip address dhcp command when issued from interface configuration mode will allow a router to obtain an IP address for that interface from a DHCP server.

In this scenario, the router is acting as a DHCP client, not a server, so the command could not be issued from dhcp-config mode. In addition, the IP address is being appointed to an interface on the router, not the router as a whole so the command could not be entered at worldwide config mode.

The most common situation in which a router interface might be set as a DHCP client is to enable one DHCP router to obtain configuration options from another router providing this service.

Consider an example where RouterA is connected to RouterB. RouterA contains a complete DHCP configuration including the options (DNS server, domain name). RouterB is connected to RouterA through its FastEthernet0 interface. The given configuration could allow RouterB to issue a different set of addresses than RouterA while importing the options from Router A. The configuration of RouterB is below as presented in the partial output of the show run command:

```
hostname RouterB
!
ip dhcp-excluded-address 40.0.0.1
ip dhcp pool B
     network 40.0.0.0 255.255.255.0
     default-router 40.0.0.1
     import all
!
interface fastethernet0
     ip address dhcp
```

Note that for this configuration to function properly, the FastEthernet0 interface on RouterB needs to be set as a DHCP client.

The command router(config)# ip address dhcp is incorrect because it is performed at the worldwide configuration prompt. The command needs to be performed in interface configuration mode.

The command router(dhcp-config)# ip address dhcp is incorrect because it is performed at the DHCP configuration prompt. The command needs to be performed in interface configuration mode.

The command router(config)# address dhcp is incorrect because it is missing the ip part of the command.

The command router(dhcp-config)# address dhcp is incorrect because it is missing the ip part of the command and it is performed at the DHCP configuration prompt. It needs to be performed in interface configuration mode.

Objective:
Layer 3 Technologies Sub-Objective:
Identify, configure, and verify IPv4 addressing and subnetting References:

Cisco > Cisco IOS IP Addressing Services Command Reference > ip address dhcp

58. Correct Answer: D

Explanation/Reference:
:
The show ip ospf neighbor [detail] command will display the OSPF information that is known about OSPF neighbors and the OSPF operating state with them.

The commands below can be used to monitor and verify OSPF operation:
- show ip ospf - shows the number of times the SPF algorithm has run and the default LSU interval.
- show ip protocol - displays information about timers, filters, metric, etc. for the entire router.
- show ip ospf database - shows the router ID, the OSPF process ID, and the contents of the topological database.

These commands do not show details about OSPF neighbors. Objective:
Layer 3 Technologies Sub-Objective:
Configure and verify OSPF neighbor relationship and verification

References:
Cisco > Cisco IOS IP Routing Protocols Command Reference > IP Routing Protocol-Independent Commands: S through T > show ip ospf neighbor

59. **Correct Answer: A**

Explanation/Reference:
:
The only loopback interface used in the communication is the loopback 0 interface of rtrA. The configuration on the rtrA router indicates that BGP is enabled on rtrA in the autonomous system number (ASN) 450. The neighbor 131.78.45.2 remote-as 450 command establishes a connection with the rtrB interface having the 131.78.45.2 address. The Gi0/1 interface of rtrB has the address 131.78.45.2, which is directly connected to the Gi0/0 interface (132.78.45.1) of rtrA. The next line, neighbor 131.78.45.2 update-source loopback 0, specifies that the 131.78.45.2 interface (Gi0/1) of rtrB communicates with the loopback 0 interface on rtrA.

In the configuration of rtrB, the neighbor 10.144.1.1 remote-as 450 command establishes a neighboring relationship with the interface having the address 10.144.1.1. The loopback 0 interface of rtrA has the address 10.144.1.1. The loopback 1 interface on rtrB is appointed an IP address but not used in establishing BGP connections among rtrA and rtrB

Loopback 1 interface of rtrB only could only be used in the communication among rtrA and rtrB if you configured rtrA and rtrB as follows:

```
rtrA(config)#router bgp 450
rtrA(config-router)# neighbor 131.78.1.1 remote-as 450

rtrB(config)#router bgp 450
rtrB(config-router)# neighbor 131.78.45.1 remote-as 450
rtrB(config-router)# neighbor 131.78.45.1 update-source loopback 1
```

Both loopback 0 and loopback 1 interfaces are NOT used for communication among rtrA and rtrB. Only the loopback 0 interface of rtrA is used. Both of the loopback interfaces could be used in the communication among rtrA and rtrB only if you changed the configuration of rtrA and rtrB, as given below:

```
rtrA(config)# router bgp 450
rtrA(config-router)# neighbor 131.78.1.1 remote-as 450
rtrA(config-router)# neighbor 131.78.1.1 update-source loopback 0

rtrB(config)#router bgp 450
rtrB(config-router)# neighbor 10.144.1.1 remote-as 450
rtrB(config-router)# neighbor 10.144.1.1 update-source loopback 1
```

Because the loopback 0 interface of rtrA is used in communication, is incorrect to state that neither loopback 0 nor loopback 1 interface is used. To ensure that neither of the loopback interfaces are be used for communication, you could configure rtrA and rtrB as follows:

```
rtrA(config)# router bgp 450
rtrA(config-router)# neighbor 131.78.45.2 remote-as 450

rtrB(config)# router bgp 450
rtrB(config-router)# neighbor 131.78.45.1 remote-as 450
```

Objective:
Layer 3 Technologies Sub-Objective:
Configure and verify eBGP (IPv4 and IPv6 address families)

References:
Cisco > Home > Support > Technology Support > IP > IP Routing > Design > Design Technotes > BGP Case Studies > eBGP Multihop Cisco > Cisco IOS IP Routing: Protocol-Independent Command Reference > neighbor update-source
Cisco > Cisco IOS IP Routing: Protocol-Independent Command Reference > neighbor remote-as

60. **Correct Answer: D**

    Explanation/Reference:
    :
    You identify the area to which a network belongs with the network area command issued from router configuration mode:

    router(config-router)# network address wildcard-mask area area-id

    To enter router configuration mode, enter the command router ospf process ID in worldwide configuration mode. For this command to be accepted and acted upon by the router, at least one interface on the router needs to have an IP address appointed and be up.

    The command router(config)# network 208.15.208.0 area 0 is incorrect because it is performed in worldwide configuration mode, as evidenced by the prompt router (config)#.

    The command router(config-if)# ip ospf area 0 is incorrect. This command could be used to configure the router for OSPF and its area. It could also enter configuration mode for that particular process of OSPF so the user can enter additional commands that affect that process. However, this command is missing the process ID.

    The command router(config)# network 208.15.208.0 255.255.255.0 area 0 is incorrect because it is performed in the wrong mode. It is entered in worldwide configuration mode instead of OSPF configuration mode. It also has an incorrect mask. You needs to use a wildcard mask instead of a regular mask in the network statements for OSPF. In this case, the mask must be 0.0.0.255 instead of 255.255.255.0.

    Objective:
    Layer 3 Technologies Sub-Objective:

    Configure and verify OSPF operations

    References:
    Cisco : OSPF Commands > network area

61. **Correct Answer: AB**

    Explanation/Reference:
    :
    The given statements are ACCURATE about the given output:
    - The 10.62.7.0 route is learned by the router through an iBGP neighbor. All five routes have been originated by an IGP.

The show ip bgp command displays information about the BGP routing table, including origin type, metric, next-hop addresses for every route learned by BGP, router ID, local preference, and BGP path. In the output, the character i in the first entry of the 10.62.7.0 destination indicates that the route was learned by an iBGP neighbor. The * symbol at the beginning of the routes indicate that they are valid routes, while the > symbol indicate that the route is the current best route.

The i at the end of the entries under the Path column indicates that the routes have been originated by an interior gateway protocol (IGP). In the scenario output, all

five routes have an i at the end of their respective entries. If the character e appears as the origin code, the routes are considered to have originated from an exterior gateway protocol (EGP). The origin code can also be the ? character, which implies that the origin of the route is unknown.

The output also displays the next-hop addresses for the routes. The 200.7.34.0 subnet is a local route, and hence has its next-hop address as 0.0.0.0.

The show ip bgp command also displays the local router's ID (RID), local preference, weight, and next-hop addresses for every route learned by BGP. In this case, the RID of RouterA is 200.17.34.15 and the local preference, weight, and next-hop address for the 10.62.7.0 network are 100, 0, and 10.62.7.78, respectively. The metric and the next-hop address for the BGP routes can also be viewed by using the show ip route bgp command, as follows:

```
RouterA# show ip route bgp
B 10.62.7.0 [200/0] via 10.62.7.78, 01:34:16
B 200.17.56.0 [200/0] via 10.62.7.78, 01:34:16
B 192.177.1.0 [20/100] via 10.62.7.115, 01:34:16
```

The BGP table version can also be displayed by using the show ip bgp neighbors and the show ip bgp summary commands. The show ip bgp neighbors command also displays the address, ASN, and RID of neighbors of the local router, as presented below:

```
RouterA# show ip bgp neighbors
BGP neighbor is 192.177.1.6, remote AS 200, external link BGP version 17,
remote router ID 200.17.34.15
BGP state = Established, table version = 16, up for 01:45:03
<output omitted>
```

The show ip bgp summary command displays the RID and the BGP table version, as presented in the given output:

```
RouterA# show ip bgp summary
BGP router identifier 200.17.34.15, local AS number 100 BGP table version is
17, main routing table version 18
<output omitted>
Neighbor V AS MsgRcvd MsgSent TblVer InQ OutQ Up/Down State/PfxRcd 10.62.7.90
17 200 56 55 18 0 0 01:42:13 27
10.62.7.145 17 300 34 33 18 0 0 00:31:20 0
```

The router is not aware of the best path for the 61.80.3.0 route. The character h appears at the beginning of the entry for the 61.80.30 destination. This means that the route is in the history state presently and that the best route is not known.

There are not four AS among the router and the 192.177.1.0 subnet. In the output, the Path column for the 192.1771.1.0 subnet lists four AS numbers. The four AS numbers refer to the ASNs traversed by the route from RouterA to the 192.177.1.0 subnet. The first AS refers to the first neighbor of RouterA; the second AS refers to the neighbor of the first neighbor; and so on. The last AS in the column is the AS of the 192.177.1.0. This implies that there are three AS (1, 2, and 3) that take place among RouterA and the subnet.

Objective:
Layer 3 Technologies

Sub-Objective:
Configure and verify eBGP (IPv4 and IPv6 address families)

References:
Cisco > Cisco IOS IP Routing: BGP Command Reference > show ip bgp Cisco > Cisco IOS IP Routing: BGP Command Reference > show ip route bgp
Cisco > Cisco IOS IP Routing: BGP Command Reference > show ip bgp summary

62. **Correct Answer: C**

    Explanation/Reference:
    :
    External BGP (eBGP) peers do update the AS_Path attribute before sending updates to another eBGP peer. This helps to maintain the path back to the source of the update.

    eBGP peers use TCP to communicate, and they do so on port 179 by default.

    Internal BGP (BGP) peers are routers that reside in the same AS. iBGP peers do not update the AS_Path attribute before sending updates to an iBGP peer. That is only done when an update is sent from an eBGP peer to another eBGP peer.

    Objective:
    Layer 3 Technologies Sub-Objective:
    Explain BGP attributes and best-path selection

    References:
    Home > About Cisco > Publications and Merchandise > The Internet Protocol Journal > Back issues > Volume 9,Number 1, March 2006 > Autonomous System Numbers > Exploring Autonomous System Numbers

63. **Correct Answer: A**

    Explanation/Reference:
    :
    The command snmp-server host 192.168.5.5 informs version 3 noauth CISCO will configure the host to authenticate a user by username and send clear text notifications. The receiver will then acknowledge receipt of the notification. The keyword informs indicates that an inform message type will be used. Unlike a trap, an inform message is acknowledged by the receiver.

    The version 3 keyword indicates that version 3 is in use, which is the ONLY version that supports verification and encryption. Finally, the noauth keyword specifies verification by username only and no encryption.

    The command snmp-server host 192.168.5.5 traps version 3 auth CISCO configures the host to send traps rather than informs.

    The command snmp-server host 192.168.5.5 informs version 2c CISCO specifies version 2c, which only support community string-based verification.

    The command snmp-server host 192.168.5.5 informs version 3 authpriv CISCO specifies the keyword authpriv, which indicates encryption will be used and verification based on HMAC-MD5 or HMAC-SHA algorithms.

    Objective: Infrastructure Services Sub-Objective:
    Configure and verify SNMP

64. Correct Answer: B

Explanation/Reference:
:
The value 30 represents the seed metric for routes that are redistributed from EIGRP into OSPF.

When configuring the OSPF process, the redistribute command is used to identify the source protocol, its AS or process ID, and several other optional parameters, such as metric. The default seed metric for all routing protocols except BGP is 20. When redistributing BGP, the default seed metric is 1.

It does not identify the seed metric associated with OSPF routes that are redistributed into EIGRP. The command is redistributing EIGRP into OSPF, not OSPF into EIGRP.

It does not identify the amount that the take placering EIGRP metric will increment as it is redistributed into OSPF. A seed metric value is an absolute value not incremental.

It does not specify that routes that contain metrics of less than 30 will be redistributed from OSPF into

EIGRP. It not used to filter routes. Objective:
Layer 3 Technologies Sub-Objective:
Configure and verify redistribution among any routing protocols or routing sources

References:
Cisco > Cisco IOS IP Routing: Protocol-Independent Command Reference > redistribute (ip)

65. Correct Answer: D
Explanation/Reference:
:
Border Gateway Protocol (BGP) routes that are redistributed into OSPF will be marked with a metric of 1 if no other metric is specified. All other routing protocols will receive a metric of 20 when redistributed into OSPF.

A metric can be manually specified when redistributing the route, as presented below:

```
router5(config)# router ospf 10
router5(config-router)# redistribute bgp 120 metric 5
```

Objective:
Layer 3 Technologies Sub-Objective:
Configure and verify redistribution among any routing protocols or routing sources

References:
Cisco Press > Articles > Network Technology > General Networking > Cisco OSPF Route Redistribution
Cisco > Support > Technology Support > IP > IP Routing > Design > Design Technotes > Redistributing Routing Protocols > Document ID: 8606

66. Correct Answer: A

Explanation/Reference:
:
The given command set could NOT be used because it only applies the access list route-map change_parameters inbound instead of outbound, as could be crucial:

```
access-list 1 permit 192.168.0.0 0.0.255.255
access-list 2 permit 172.161.94.0 0.0.0.255
router bgp 505
neighbor 201.60.3.1 remote-as 501
neighbor 201.60.3.1 route-map change_parameters in
```

The following commands should be used to configure BGP on rtrB as desired:

```
access-list 1 permit 192.168.0.0 0.0.255.255
access-list 2 permit 172.161.94.0 0.0.0.255
router bgp 505
neighbor 201.60.3.1 remote-as 501
neighbor 201.60.3.1 route-map change_parameters out

route-map change_parameters permit 10
match ip-address 2
set metric 500

route-map change_parameters permit 20
match ip-address 1
set metric 300
```

The following set of commands creates two standard access-lists numbered 1 and 2:

```
access-list 1 permit 192.168.0.0 0.0.255.255
access-list 2 permit 172.161.94.0 0.0.0.255
router bgp 505
neighbor 201.60.3.1 remote-as 501
neighbor 201.60.3.1 route-map change_parameters out
```

The ACL 1 allows the 192.168.58.0/24 and the 192.168.127.0/24 subnets, while the ACL 2 allows the 172.161.94.0/24 subnet. The neighbor route-map command specifies a route-map named change_parameters for the 201.60.3.1 BGP peer. The out keyword at the end of the command indicates that the route-map is applied only to the updates sent by rtrB, and not received by rtrB.

In the given command, the route map change_parameters is defined with the permit keyword. The permit keyword indicates that if a match take places, the actions specified in the set sub-command are performed:

route-map change_parameters permit 10 match ip-address 2
set metric 500

In this case, this command checks if the IP address of the subnets advertised to rtrA is in the 172.161.94.0/24 subnet (specified by ACL 2). If the IP address matches, then the metric of those routes are set to 500.

In the given command, the route map change_parameters is defined with the permit keyword:

route-map change_parameters permit 20 match ip-address 1
set metric 300

In this case, this command checks if the IP address of the subnets advertised to rtrA is in the 192.168.58.0/24 or the 192.168.127.0/24 subnets (specified by ACL 1) If the IP address matches, then the metric of those routes are set to 300.

Objective:
Layer 3 Technologies Sub-Objective:
Configure and verify eBGP (IPv4 and IPv6 address families)

References:
Cisco > Home > Support > Technology Support > IP > IP Routing > Design > Design Technotes > BGP

Case Studies > Route Maps Cisco > Cisco IOS IP Routing: Protocol-Independent Command Reference > route-map

67. **Correct Answer:** BD
    Explanation/Reference:
    :
    For non-ISP autonomous systems (AS), redistribution into IGP is crucial when BOTH of the given
    - conditions take place: Not all routers run BGP
    - Knowledge of external routes is crucial inside the AS

    Note: Redistribution of any BGP routes into your IGP can cause serious issues, even if your internal routers can handle the load. This must be done rarely, if at

    all. If you do decide to do this, configure heavy filtering to allow only very few routes into OSPF or EIGRP so as not to overwhelm those protocols. For instance, do it only for a select group of networks for which optimal routing is critical.

    Objective:
    Layer 3 Technologies Sub-Objective:
    Configure and verify redistribution among any routing protocols or routing sources

    References:
    Cisco > Support > Technology Support > IP > IP Routing > Design > Design Technotes > BGP Case Studies > Document ID: 26634 > Static Routes and Redistribution
    Cisco > Cisco IOS IP Routing: BGP Configuration Guide, Release 12.4 > Cisco BGP Overview > Information About Cisco BGP > BGP Autonomous Systems

68. **Correct Answer:** C

    Explanation/Reference:
    :
    The correct answer is show ip ospf virtual-links. The show ip ospf virtual-links command displays the current state of OSPF virtual links, as presented below.

    ```
    Router10# show ip ospf virtual-links
    Virtual Link to router 192.168.15.7 is up
    Transit area 0.0.0.1, via interface Ethernet1, Cost of using 10
    Transmit Delay is 1 sec, State POINT_TO_POINT
    Timer intervals configured, Hello 10, Dead 40, Wait 40, Retransmit 5
    Hello due in 0:00:08
    Adjacency State FULL
    ```

    The given additional commands are available to verify OSPF configurations: show ip ospf border-routers,

    debug ip ospf adj, and show ip ospf. The show ip ospf border-routers command displays internal OSPF

    routing table entries for an ABR, as presented below.

    ```
    router10#show ip ospf border-routers
    Codes: i - Intra-area route, I-Inter-area route

    Type Dest Address Cost NextHop Interface ABR ASBR Area SPF i 2.2.2.2 10
    192.1.1.199 Ethernet 2 ACCURATE INACCURATE 0 3
    i 3.2.2.2 10 192.1.1.200 Ethernet 2 ACCURATE INACCURATE 0 3
    ```

    The show ip ospf command displays information about the router's role and each area to which the router is connected, as presented below.

```
router10# show ip ospf
Routing Process "ospf 3" with ID 15.0.0.1 and Domain ID 15.20.0.1
Supports only single TOS(TOS0) routes
Supports opaque LSA
SPF schedule delay 5 secs, Hold time between two SPFs 10 secs
Minimum LSA interval 5 secs. Minimum LSA arrival 1 secs
LSA group pacing timer 100 secs
Interface flood pacing timer 55 msecs
Retransmission pacing timer 100 msecs
Number of external LSA 0. Checksum Sum 0x0
Number of opaque AS LSA 0. Checksum Sum 0x0
Number of DCbitless external and opaque AS LSA 0
Number of DoNotAge external and opaque AS LSA 0
Number of areas in this router is 2. 2 normal 0 stub 0 nssa
External flood list length 0
Area BACKBONE(0)
Number of interfaces in this area is 3
Area has message digest authentication
SPF algorithm executed 4 times
Area ranges are
Number of LSA 4. Checksum Sum 0x29BEB
Number of opaque link LSA 0. Checksum Sum 0x0
Number of DCbitless LSA 3
Number of indication LSA 0
Number of DoNotAge LSA 0
Flood list length 0
Area 172.16.40.0
Number of interfaces in this area is 0
Area has no authentication
SPF algorithm executed 1 times
Area ranges are
192.168.0.0/16 Passive Advertise
Number of LSA 1. Checksum Sum 0x44FD
Number of opaque link LSA 0. Checksum Sum 0x0
Number of DCbitless LSA 1
Number of indication LSA 1
Number of DoNotAge LSA 0
Flood list length 0
```

The debug ip ospf adj command displays information about the state of neighbor adjacencies, as presented below.

R3#debug ip ospf adj
OSPF adjacency events debugging is on

```
00:54:04: OSPF: Rcv pkt from 172.12.23.2, Ethernet0, area 0.0.0.1 : src not on
the same network
```

In the above example, either the IP address or the subnet mask is misconfigured on either this router or

the neighbor. Objective:
Layer 3 Technologies
Sub-Objective:
Configure and verify network types, area types, and router types

References:
Cisco > Cisco IOS IP Routing Protocols Command Reference > IP Routing Protocol-Independent Commands: S through T > show ip ospf virtual-links

69. Correct Answer: A

Explanation/Reference:
:
The value 4294967295 in the debug ip eigrp output represents the unreachable metric for EIGRP. This means that the network has become unavailable and cannot be reached. In this output, the M represents the local metric, and the SM represents the metric that was reported by the neighbor that advertised the network to the local router.

The administrative distance (AD) for internal EIGRP is 90.

The link features that are used in the EIGRP calculation are presented given the dash after the M and SM values (1657856 4294967295). By default, EIGRP only uses bandwidth and delay in its calculation.

Objective:
Layer 3 Technologies Sub-Objective:
Define and optimize EIGRP metrics

References:
Cisco > Cisco IOS Debug Command Reference > debug h225 asn1 through debug ip ftp > debug ip eigrp

70. Correct Answer: FG

Explanation/Reference:
:
The R2 router will not form adjacencies with neighboring routers in the area if the area IDs do not match. The area keyword in the network command is missing from the initial router R2 configuration. The correct command could be:

R2(config)# network 192.16.31.0 0.0.0.255 area 1

Secondly, the subnets keyword must be used in the redistribute command to ensure that all of the subnets in the 10.0.0.0/8 are redistributed into OSPF. For example, you could use the given commands to redistribute EIGRP autonomous system (AS) 50 networks and subnetworks into OSPF with a metric of 100 and advertise them as external Type 1 routes:

R2(config)# router ospf
R2(config-router)# redistribute eigrp 50 metric 100 metric-type 1

The complete syntax for the redistribute command when used in OSPF is as follows:

redistribute protocol [process-id] [metric metric-value] [metric-type type-value] [subnets]

The command parameters are:

- protocol - Identifies the source protocol, such as BGP, connected, EIGRP, IGRP, ISIS, OSPF, static,
- or rip. process-id - Depending on the routing protocol, identifies the source autonomous system
- number or process ID. metric - Identifies the seed metric for the redistributed route. The default is 0.
- metric-type - For OSPF, it identifies the redistributed routes as either external Type 1 or Type 2 routes. The default is Type 2. subnets - Optional keyword for use with OSPF to indicate that the scope of the networks to be redistributed also includes subnets.

Objective:
Layer 3 Technologies Sub-Objective:
Configure and verify redistribution among any routing protocols or routing sources

References:
Cisco > Cisco IOS IP Routing: Protocol-Independent Command Reference > redistribute (ip)

71. Correct Answer: B

Explanation/Reference:
:
When EIGRP loses it best route, called the successor route, it will then use a feasible successor route, if available, to route the packets to that destination. To be considered a feasible successor, the advertised distance, which is the neighboring router's distance, needs to be less than the feasible distance, which is the local router's own metric.

In this scenario, the feasible distance is 3. The only available feasible successors are the ones that have

the advertised distance/feasible distance of 1/4 and 2/4. Objective:
Layer 3 Technologies Sub-Objective:
Configure and verify policy-based routing

References:
Cisco > Home > Support > Technology Support > IP Routing > Technology Information > Technology White Paper > Enhanced Interior Gateway Routing Protocol > Feasible Distance, Reported Distance, and Feasible Successor

72. **Correct Answer:** C

    Explanation/Reference:
    :
    The effect of the passive-interface command is dependent on the routing protocol. With RIP, the command prevents the sending of route updates, but does not prevent the reception of route updates. With EIGRP, the passive-interface command prevents both the sending and receiving of route updates, and also the sending of hellos. Without hello packets, the routers are unable to maintain the neighbor relationship, upon which all communications including route updates depend.

    If the intent was to preventing routing updates from Router 1 to Router 2 while still allowing updates from Router 2 to Router 1, the routing updates needs to be filtered out and denied on Router 1 with a distribute list, as presented in the given command set:

    router1(config)access-list 101 deny any router1(config)#router eigrp 100 router1(config-router)distribute-list 101 out

    Objective:
    Layer 3 Technologies Sub-Objective:
    Troubleshoot passive interfaces

    References:
    Cisco IOS Master Command List, Release 12.4T > p through r > passive-interface
    Cisco > Home > Support > Technology Support > IP > IP Routing > Design > Design Technotes > Filtering Routing Updates on Distance Vector IP Routing Protocols

73. **Correct Answer:** AB
    Explanation/Reference:
    :
    The effect of the passive-interface command is dependent on the routing protocol running on the interface. For EIGRP, the router will not only stop sending routing updates, but also hellos, which means that it will not form a neighbor relationship with another EIGRP router on that interface. This is also the case with OSPF and IS-IS. With RIP, however, the router will continue to send hellos even as it stops sending routing updates, and it will still receive routing updates. An example of using the passive-interface command is below. The command is issued from the router configuration mode.

    ```
    Router(config-router)# passive-interface ethernet 0/0
    ```

    The passive-interface command will even overrule a configuration that includes a distribute list that allows the advertisement of a network through the interface. inspect the partial output of the show run command taken from a router running EIGRP below:

```
router6#show run
!
router eigrp 100
network 10.16.18.0 0.0.255.255
network 10.16.19.0 0.0.255.255
passive-interface serial 0/0 distribute-list 50 out serial 0/0
!
Access-list 50 permit 10.16.8.0 0.0.255.255
```

In this case, although the distribute list allows the advertisement of the 10.16.8.0 network, the passive-interface command applied to the Serial 0/0 interface will disallow all outgoing and incoming updates.

The passive-interface command does not affect the transmission or reception of normal data traffic, only routing updates.

The passive-interface command does not disable the router interface. The shutdown command is used to

disable a router interface. The passive-interface command does not place the router in standby mode.

Objective:
Layer 3 Technologies Sub-Objective:
Configure and verify loop prevention mechanisms

References:
Cisco > Home > Support > Technology Support > IP > IP Routing > Design > Design Technotes > How Does the Passive Interface Feature Work in EIGRP?
Cisco > Cisco IOS IP Routing: Protocol-Independent Configuration Guide, Release 12.4 > Configuring IP Routing Protocol-Independent Features > Filtering Routing Information
Cisco > Cisco IOS IP Routing: Protocol-Independent Command Reference > passive-interface

74. **Correct Answer:** AB

Explanation/Reference:
:
ABRs generate Type 3 and Type 4 LSAs in an OSPF network. ABRs are those routers that take place among two OSPF areas, as presented in the given figure:

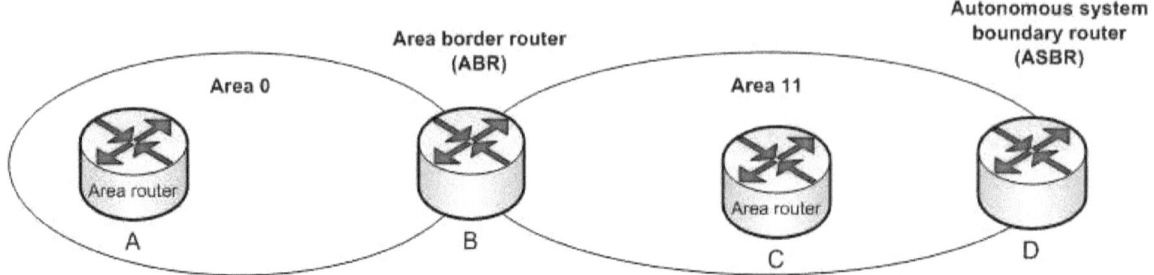

Type 3 and Type 4 LSAs are generated by ABRs to be flooded into other areas to and from the backbone area (area 0). Type 3 LSAs, or summary link advertisements, contain the list of networks known by one area. ABRs send Type 3 LSAs to the other OSPF areas in a given AS.

OSPF ABRs generates Type 4 LSAs to advertise the list of routes that point to an ASBR. These LSAs advertise the location of the ASBR.

Type 5 LSAs are not generated by an ABR. These LSAs are generated by ASBRs to define routes redistributed into the area from other autonomous systems.

Type 2 LSAs are not generated by an ABR. A Type 2 LSA is generated only by the designated router (DR) of a segment to be sent to the other routers that belong to the same area as the DR. A DR is a router that has the highest OSPF priority on a segment. These advertisements are used by the DR to represent the routers that are connected to the network.

Objective:
Layer 3 Technologies Sub-Objective:

Configure and verify network types, area types, and router types

References:
Cisco Learning Home > Groups > CCNP R&S Study Group > Discussions > OSPF Level of Detail
Cisco > Support > Technology Support > IP > IP Routing > Technology Information > Technology White Paper > OSPF Design Guide > Link State Packets

75. Correct Answer: D

Explanation/Reference:
:
Issuing the given commands will cause RTR2 to advertise the CIDR block 192.168.0.0/16 to the other routers by using BGP:

```
RTR2(config)# router bgp 65100
RTR2(config-router)# neighbor 172.16.1.2 remote-as 65101
RTR2(config-router)# neighbor 192.168.3.2 remote-as 65100
RTR2(config-router)# network 192.168.0.0 mask 255.255.0.0
RTR2(config-router)# ip route 192.168.0.0 255.255.0.0 null 0
```

The network command specifies the address that will be inserted into the BGP table. Without the mask keyword, the classful network will be assumed. Because 255.255.0.0, or /16, is not the natural mask for any Class C address, the mask keyword needs to also be specified. Thus, 192.168.0.0 and 255.255.0.0 identify the desired address and mask of the 192.168.0.0/16 network prefix.

The router checks the IP forwarding table for an exact match before it advertises the route. Without a matching entry in the IP forwarding table, that route will not be advertised. RTR2 needs to be able to advertise a CIDR block and not the individual subnets. A static route is crucial because BGP requires that a match of the network prefix be present in the forwarding table when using the network command with the mask keyword. Therefore, to ensure an exact match for the identified prefix take places in the IP forwarding table, and to ensure that the prefix will always be advertised, a static route for 192.168.0.0/16 to null 0 is also crucial.

The syntax for the network command is presented below:

network network-number [mask network-mask] [route-map map-tag]

The parameters are:
- mask - This parameter is optional and identifies the network or subnetwork to advertise.
- route-map - This parameter is optional and identifies a preconfigured route-map that will be used to filter specific addresses from being advertised.

The given command set is missing the mask keyword in the network command and the command to create a static route to null 0. The address used in the network command is also incorrect. It must 192.168.0.0:

router bgp 65100
neighbor 172.16.1.2 remote-as 65100
neighbor 192.168.3.2 remote-as 65100
network 192.168.3.0

The given command set is missing the mask keyword in the network command and the command to create a static route to null 0:

router bgp 65100

neighbor 172.16.1.2 remote-as 65101
neighbor 192.168.3.2 remote-as 65100
network 192.168.0.0

The given command set uses an incorrect mask (255.0.0.0) in the command that creates the static route to null 0. It must be 255.255.0.0:

router bgp 65100
neighbor 172.16.1.2 remote-as 65100
neighbor 192.168.3.2 remote-as 65100
network 192.168.0.0 mask 255.255.0.0
ip route 192.0.0.0 255.0.0.0 null 0

Objective:
Layer 3 Technologies Sub-Objective:
Define, configure, and verify BGP peer relationships and verification

References:
Internetworking Case Studies > Using the Border Gateway Protocol for Interdomain Routing > Controlling the Flow of BGP Updates > CIDR and Aggregate Addresses > Aggregation and Static Routes

76. Correct Answer: C

Explanation/Reference:

The show ip bgp neighbors command will show you detailed information about all of the router's neighbors or peers. A sample of the show ip bgp neighbors output is presented below. The sample utilizes the ip address parameter, which is optional, but can used to limit the output to display information about only one neighbor:

```
Router15# show ip bgp neighbors 10.5.1.6

BGP neighbor is 10.5.1.6, remote AS 11, internal link
BGP version 4, remote router ID 10.1.5.6
BGP state = Active, table version 0
Last read 00:00:12, hold time is 180, keepalive interval is 60 seconds
Minimum time between advertisement runs is 30 seconds
Received 19 messages, 0 notifications, 0 in queue
Sent 17 messages, 0 notifications, 0 in queue
Inbound path policy configured
Route map for incoming advertisements is testing
Connections established 2; dropped 1
Connection state is ESTAB, I/O status: 1, unread input bytes: 0
Local host: 10.5.1.7, Local port: 11002
Foreign host: 10.5.1.6, Foreign port: 179

<output omitted>
```

In the above example, router15 has sent out a BGP open packet to the peer at 10.5.1.6 and is listening for a connection request from the peer. This can be defined by the line that says BGP state = Active. It can also be defined that router has established a TCP connection two times, as evidenced by the line Connections established 2.

The show ip bgp command displays the contents of the BGP routing table. It will not display detailed information about a router's BGP connections to neighboring routers.

The show ip bgp summary command displays a summary of the status of BGP connections. It will not display detailed information about a router's BGP connections to neighboring routers.

There is no show ip bgp connections command. Objective:
Layer 3 Technologies Sub-Objective:

Define, configure, and verify BGP peer relationships and verification

References:
Cisco IOS Master Command List, Release 12.4 > a through b > BGP Commands: show ip through T > show ip bgp neighbors

77. Correct Answer: C

Explanation/Reference:
:
The 3 in the area range command specifies the area that contains the routes that are to be summarized. In OSPF, you can only configure summarization on the border routers. The summaries need to be of routes within a single area. You summarize the routes of an area so that routers in another area do not see the individual networks, just the summary. The correct command syntax is presented below:

area number range ip-address mask

The number parameter is the number of the area whose networks are being summarized. For example, in the network presented in the graphic below, to summarize the networks within area 2 to 10.1.0.0/16, you could configure router A with the command area 2 range 10.1.0.0 255.255.0.0. This could not affect the routing tables of the routers within area 2, but instead make the routing tables of areas 0 and 1 smaller. These other routers could only have the summary route listed instead of the individual networks. Router C could only see the summary route 10.1.0.0/16.

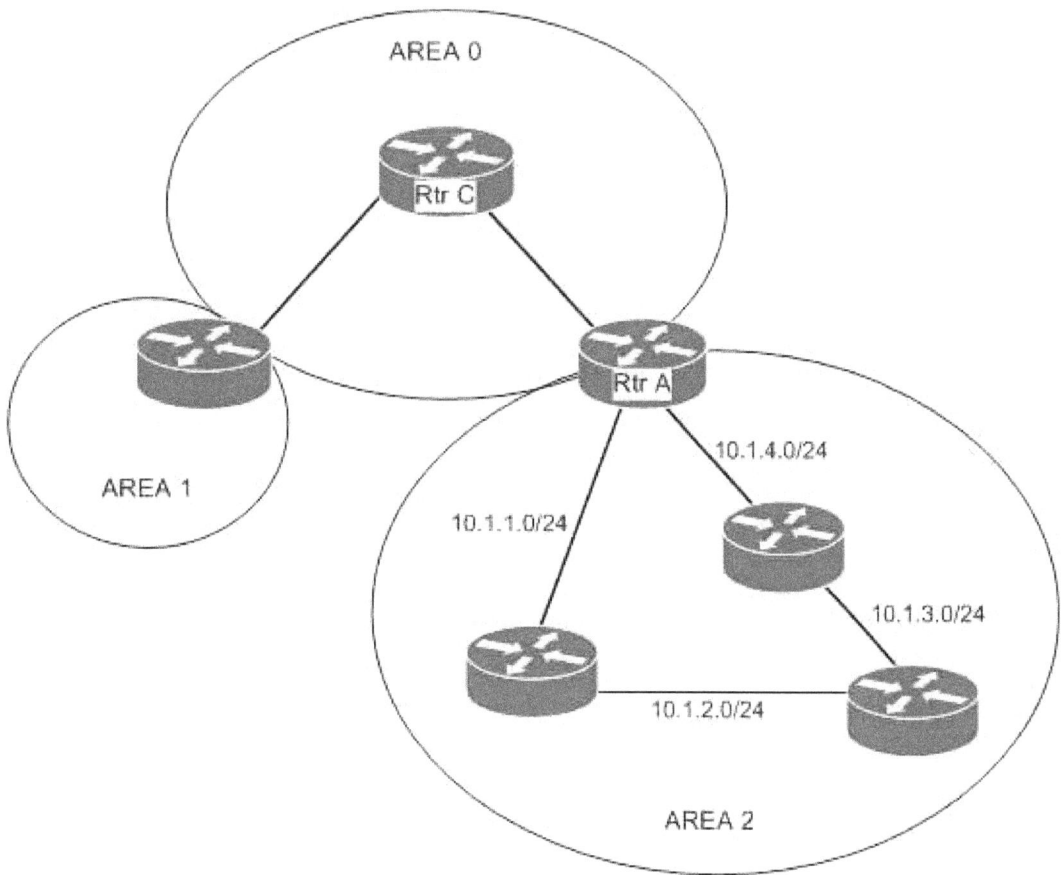

Objective:
Layer 3 Technologies Sub-Objective:
Configure and verify manual and autosummarization with any routing protocol

References:
Cisco IOS Master Command Reference > a through b > area range

78. Correct Answer: D
Explanation/Reference:
:

The show ipv6 interface command is used to verify the link-local, worldwide unicast, and multicast addresses appointed to an IPv6-enabled router interface. The show ipv6 interface command displays information regarding that interface, such as the physical state, MTU, and IPv6 enable/disable state.

A partial output of the show ipv6 interface command on an IPv6-enabled router named rtrA is as follows:

```
rtrA# show ipv6 interface FastEthernet 0/1
FastEthernet0/1 is up, line protocol is up
  IPv6 is enabled, link-local address is FE80::6339:7BFF:FE5D:A031/64
  Global unicast address(es):
    2001:7067:90D1:1::1, subnet is 2001:7067:90D1:1/64
  Joined group address(es):
    FF02::1
    FF02::2
    FF02::1:FF5D:A031
  MTU is 1500 bytes
  <output omitted>
```

In the given sample output, you can see that the Fa0/1 interface of rtrA has the link-local address FE80::6339:7BFF:FE5D:A031/64 and the worldwide unicast address 2001:7067:90D1:1::1. The worldwide unicast address is not in EUI-64 format because when the ipv6 address command was issued, the eui64 keyword was not used. If EUI-64 format had been specified with the eui64 keyword, the worldwide unicast address could have been 2001:7067:90D1:1:6339:7BFF:FE5D:A031.

An IPv6-enabled interface has not only a link-local and worldwide unicast address, but also one or more multicast addresses. A multicast address is an IPv6 address that has the prefix FF00::/8. These addresses are appointed to interfaces of different nodes such that they appear as a logical group. This implies that when a packet is destined for a multicast address, that packet is delivered to all the interfaces that have the same multicast address. The various multicast groups are as follows:

- FF02::1 Indicates the group of all the nodes on the local segment FF02::2 Indicates the group of all the routers on the local segment
- FF02::1:FF00:0/104 Indicates a solicited-node multicast group for every unicast or anycast address appointed to the interface

You can also notice in the sample output that the Fa0/1 interface belongs to three multicast groups: FF02::1, FF02::2, and FF02::1:FF5D:A031. The first two multicast groups refer to the all-host and all-router multicast groups, respectively. The third group, FF02::1:FF5D:A031, is the solicited-node multicast address. This

address is created for every unicast or anycast address. A solicited-node multicast address is defined by assigning the least significant 24 bits of the unicast address to the least significant 24 bits of the FF02::1:FF00:0 address.

The show ipv6 neighbors command displays the link-local /worldwide unicast addresses of the neighbors, including other information such as state and the next-hop interface.

The show ipv6 route command is used to view the IPv6 routing table on the router. This command displays the prefixes, administrative distance, metric, and next- hop addresses for various IPv6 networks.

The show ipv6 protocols command is used to view the active routing protocols for IPv6 on the router. This command shows the interfaces, redistribution status, and summarization status about each of the routing protocols enabled on the router.

Objective:
Layer 3 Technologies Sub-Objective:
Identify IPv6 addressing and subnetting

References:

Cisco IOS IPv6 Command Reference > show ipv6 eigrp topology through show ipv6 nat statistics > show ipv6 interface Cisco IOS IPv6 Command Reference > show ipv6 nat translations through show ipv6 protocols > show ipv6 neighbors Cisco IOS IPv6 Command Reference > show ipv6 nat translations through show ipv6 protocols > show ipv6 protocols
Cisco > Products & Services > Cisco IOS and NX-OS Software > Cisco IOS Technologies > IPv6 > Product Literature > White Papers > Cisco IOS IPv6 Multicast Introduction
Cisco > IPv6 Execution Guide, Release 15.2M&T > Executing IPv6 Multicast

79. Correct Answer: B
Explanation/Reference:
:
The ipv6 enable command must be used on R1 to enable IPv6. This command automatically provides an IPv6 link-local unicast address for the interface on which IPv6 is being configured. If an explicit IPv6 address were configured on the interface, the command could not be crucial.

The ipv6 router ospf command must not be used in the configuration because this command allows you to

enter the router configuration mode for OSPF for IPv6. The ipv6 ospf neighbor command is used to

configure neighboring routers for OSPF.

The ipv6 ospf cost command must not be added to the configuration because this command allows you to specify the OSPF cost to send packets from a given interface.

Objective:
Layer 3 Technologies Sub-Objective:
Configure and verify OSPF for IPv6

References:
  Cisco > Cisco IOS IPv6 Command Reference > ipv6 enable

80. Correct Answer: A

Explanation/Reference:
:
The output of the command shows that Router C and Router B will fail to have all OSPF routes in their tables. In a hub and spoke configuration, as depicted in the diagram, the hub router (Router A) must be the designated router (DR) or the source of updates to the other routers. However, Router B is the DR, as evidenced by the output of the show ip ospf neighbor command performed on Router A.

This situation could be rectified by setting Routers B and C with a priority of 0, which could disqualify them from being the DR. After that, all routes could be

distributed from the hub, which could have visibility of all routes.

All routing tables will be populated correctly until the hub router is made the DR.

Neither Router A nor C will be the DR, since it is indicated that Router B is the DR in the output of the

command. Objective:
Layer 3 Technologies Sub-Objective:
Configure and verify OSPF operations

References:
Cisco > Home > Support > Support Technology > Support > IP Routing > Configure > Configuration Examples and Technotes > Initial Configurations for OSPF over Frame Relay Subinterfaces
Cisco > Cisco IOS Wide-Area Networking Command Reference > frame-relay lapf n201 through fr-atm connect dlci > frame-relay map Cisco > Cisco IOS IP Routing: OSPF Command Reference > ip ospf network

81. Correct Answer: C

Explanation/Reference:
:
Next Hop Resolution Protocol (NHRP) allows the spoke routers to register their IP addresses with the NHRP server, which is the hub router. It also allows the spoke routers to then learn the physical IP addresses of the other spoke routers from the hub router, allowing for GRE links to be built dynamically as needed among the spokes. This eliminates the need for the traffic to go through the hub router.

Dynamic Multipoint VPN (DMVPN) technology leverages the given associated technologies:
    IPsec mGRE
    Dynamic routing protocols NHRP
    Cisco Express Forwarding

It makes it conceivable to build the hub router once, and add spokes later, making no additional changes to the hub. The spokes are able to register with the hub and dynamically build their own connections to other spokes using the IP addresses learned from the hub using NHRP. DMVPN also allows IPsec point-to-point GRE tunnels to be built to new spokes with no IPsec peering configuration. The multipoint GRE technology (mGRE) allows a single physical interface on the hub to be used for all spoke connections.

Finally, the routing protocols used by DMVPN allow the routers to share routing information, while Cisco Express Forwarding (CEF) is a switching technology that improves performance while reducing the load on the CPUs of the routers.

Objective:
VPN Technologies Sub-Objective:
Define DMVPN (single hub)

References:
Cisco > Dynamic Multipoint VPN (DMVPN) Design Guide (Version 1.1) > DMVPN Design Overview

82. Correct Answer: AE

Explanation/Reference:
:
The interface ID of the subinterface created to host the virtual network named red will be FastEthernet1/0/0.3, and the IP address will be 10.1.1.1.

When a virtual routing and forwarding (VRF) instance is defined, it will have a name and a tag number. The tag number is used by the router to dynamically create a subinterface on the specified physical interface of the EVN trunk. The tag number is appended to the physical interface ID. Since the virtual network (vnet) trunk was defined as FastEthernet1/0/0, the subinterface for vrf red will be FastEthernet1/0/0.3. All subinterfaces on the trunk will use the same IP address as the physical interface defined as the trunk.

Easy virtual networking (EVN) is a technology that allows for multiple logical networks to use the same physical infrastructure. EVN trunks carry the traffic of multiple VRFs. While the subinterfaces dedicated to each VRF use the same IP address (that of the physical interface of the EVN trunk), no IP address conflicts ever take place because each VRF maintains its own routing and forwarding tables, and while on the trunk, each uses a VRF tag to separate the traffic from each VRF.

Objective:
VPN Technologies Sub-Objective:
Define Easy Virtual Networking (EVN)

References:
Cisco > Easy Virtual Network Configuration Guide, Cisco IOS XE Release 3S > Overview of Easy Virtual Network

83. Correct Answer: A

Explanation/Reference:
:
The interface needs to be able to support 802.1q encapsulation. The EVN trunk carries the traffic of multiple virtual routing and forwarding (VRF) instances, with the traffic of each instance tagged with an ID called the virtual network tag. Since the VLAN ID field of an 802.1q encapsulated packet is used for this ID, the link needs to be one that supports 802.1q.

Easy Virtual networking is a technology that allows for the creation of separate networks with separate routing tables and routing instances using the same physical topology. The IP addressing for the networks can even overlap with no issue. The networks are kept separate using the network ID tags in a similar fashion to the way switches keep VLANs separate by using VLAN tags.

An EVN trunk interface cannot also be configured for VRF-Lite. VRF-Lite is an earlier technology that

accomplishes the same goal, but lacks the simplicity of EVN. Neither RIP nor OSPFv3 is supported in

Easy Virtual Networking EVN at all.

Objective:
VPN Technologies Sub-Objective:
Define Easy Virtual Networking (EVN)

References:
Cisco > Easy Virtual Network Configuration Guide, Cisco IOS XE Release 3S > Overview of Easy Virtual Network

84. Correct Answer: C

Explanation/Reference:
:
The mapping was created through an NHRP registration request, as indicated by the flag setting registered. Next Hop Resolution Protocol (NHRP) can be used in place of static IP address to NBMA address mappings to allow the spoke routers in an mGRE hub-and-spoke configuration to discover one another's physical IP addresses.

When the output of the show nhrp detail command shows the registered flag listed, it means that the mapping was created dynamically and was learned through a registration request to the next hop server (NHS).

The mapping was not created statically. Had it been created statically, the Type field could not be listed as dynamic. It could say static.

The NHRP information DID come from the next hop server (NHS). That is indicated by the presence of the authoritative flag. The NHS is the next hop to the destination as indicated by the routing table.

The device at 10.1.1.2 is not necessarily behind a NAT router. The presence of the nat flag in the output indicates that the device at 10.1.1.2 supports the NHRP NAT extension type for supporting dynamic spoke-to-spoke tunnels to or from spokes behind a NAT router. This flag does not mean that the spoke (NHS client) is behind a NAT router.

Objective:
VPN Technologies Sub-Objective:
Define DMVPN (single hub)

References:
Home > Support > Product support > Cisco IOS and NX-OS software > Cisco IOS software releases 12.4 mainline > Configure > Feature Guides > NHRP

85. Correct Answer: C

Explanation/Reference:
:
It will drop the packet. The partial output of the show run command shows that the ip verify unicast source reachable via rx command has been performed on the Serial 0/0 interface. This enables the Unicast Reverse Path Forwarding (Unicast RPF) feature. This feature prevents IP spoofing by verifying from the routing table that there is a valid return path to the source IP address. If there is not valid return path, you can assume the IP address has been spoofed. When the command ends in the keyword rx, it means that there needs to be a return path through the interface where the command was performed. This is called strict mode.

The packet arrived on the Serial0/0 interface. The routing table shows that there is no routing entry for the 192.168.5.0/24 network that leads back through the entry interface of Serial0/0. In fact, in this instance there is no routing table entry for that network leading to any interface. When this take places, the router will drop the

packet.

The router will not send the packet to either the Ethernet0/0 or the Tunnel0 interfaces because the destination network, 10.11.11.0/24, is not a reachable destination on those interfaces. Even if it were reachable, the Unicast Reverse Path Forwarding (Unicast RPF) feature will drop the packet because it has been spoofed.

It will not send the packet to the Ethernet0/1 interface. The Unicast Reverse Path Forwarding (Unicast RPF) feature will drop the packet because it has been spoofed. If the packet were not spoofed, it could be sent to the Ethernet0/1 interface because that is the interface used by the default route. Because there is no route in the table to the 10.11.11.0/24 network, it could be sent to the default route.

Objective:
Infrastructure Security Sub-Objective:
Configure and verify router security features

References:
Cisco IOS Security Configuration Guide, Release 12.2 > Configuring Unicast Reverse Path Forwarding
Cisco > Configuring Unicast Reverse Path Forwarding

86. Correct Answer: BE

Explanation/Reference:
:
There are two contributors to the CPU load increase from ACL logging: process switching of packets that match log-enabled access control entries (ACEs), and the generation and transmission of the log messages. To reduce the impact of process switched traffic, the ip access-list logging interval command can be used. The

interval is specified in milliseconds and represents how often a single packet is process switched. While the messages in the generated log entries may not be as comprehensive after this command is performed, the counter values that are generated by the show access-list and show ip-access list commands will still be accurate.

Packets that are not process switched (CEF switched and fast switched) will examined or accounted for in the logging, so they are not the source of the issue.

The ip access-list log-update threshold command is used to configure how often syslog messages are generated and sent after the initial packet match. While this could be a beneficial command to run, as it addresses the second source of CPU congestion that is the sending of the syslog messages, that was not listed as a traffic type option. Therefore, this could not be a solution to the issue presented by packet switched traffic.

The logging rate limit command also will reduce the impact of log generation and transmission on the

CPU, but again, it does not address the issue presented by process switched traffic.

Objective:
Infrastructure Security Sub-Objective:
Configure and verify router security features

References:
Understanding Access Control List Logging
Cisco > Cisco IOS Security Command Reference: Commands D to L > ip-group

87. Correct Answer: B
Explanation/Reference:
:
The list is applied to the wrong interface. An access list that is designed to control remote access must be applied to the VTY lines, not to one of the physical interfaces. If the command were formatted correctly, the show run output could appear as follows:

```
<output omitted>

ipv6 access-list secureaccess
permit ipv6 host 2001:DB8:0:4::32 any eq ssh

line vty 0 14
ipv6 access-class secureaccess in
<output omitted>

FastEthernet0/0/1
```

The IPv6 address is formatted correctly. Although it has been shortened in format, it follows all of the shortening rules. It omits only leading zeros and it utilizes the double colon only once.

The access list does not require a deny statement. There is an implicit deny all at the end of the list.

The ipv6 access-group command must not be used to apply the list. This command is used when an access list is applied to a physical interface, not the VTY lines.

Objective:
Infrastructure Security Sub-Objective:
Configure and verify router security features

References:
Cisco > IPv6 Configuration Guide, Cisco IOS Release 15.0S > Executing Traffic Filters and Firewalls for IPv6 Security > Access Control Lists for IPv6 Traffic
Filtering
Cisco > Security Configuration Guide: Access Control Lists, Cisco IOS Release 15S > Controlling Access to a Virtual Terminal Line

88. Correct Answer: B

Explanation/Reference:
:
The command ip cef needs to be present in the configuration to support Unicast Reverse Path Forwarding (RPF). If the router is set to its defaults, it will be present. Unicasts RPF uses the tables created by CEF to validate packet source addresses. Therefore, it needs to be enabled. Unicast RPF can be enabled in three modes:

- Strict mode - The source address needs to be needs to be reachable on the interface where the packet arrived.
- Loose mode - Traffic is allowed if the source address is reachable via any interface on the router as indicted in the routing table. VRF mode - Evaluates an incoming packet's source IP address against

the VRF table configured for an eBGP neighbor.

The bandwidth command, while desirable to ensure proper cost calculation of the interface for routing purposes, is not a necessitate for Unicast RPF. The ip route 0.0.0.0 0.0.0.0 command creates a default route. A default route does not need to be present for Unicast RPF to function.

The log command is not crucial. This command must be used with caution with any access list, as it causes an increase in CPU usage in the router.

Objective:
Infrastructure Security Sub-Objective:
Configure and verify router security features

References:
Cisco IOS Security Configuration Guide, Release 12.2 > Part 5: Other Security Features > Configuring Unicast Reverse Path Forwarding Cisco > Cisco IOS IP Switching Command Reference > ip cef

89. Correct Answer: C

Explanation/Reference:
:
The auth keyword specifies that the user must be authenticated using either the HMAC-MD5 or HMAC-SHA algorithms. These algorithms are specified during the creation of the SNMP user.

For example, the given command creates a user named V3User that will be a member of the SNMP group V3Group and will use HMAC-MD5 with a password of MyPassword:

snmp-server user V3User V3Group v3 auth md5 MyPassword

The verification mechanism is not configured on the interface. All SNMP commands are performed at the worldwide configuration prompt.

The verification mechanism is not configured at the host level. The version and security model (verification, verification and encryption, or neither) are set at the host level.

The verification mechanism is not configured at the SNMP group level. The group level is where access permissions like read and write are set. This is why a user account needs to be a member of a group to derive an access level, even if it is a group of one.

Objective:
Infrastructure Services Sub-Objective:
Configure and verify SNMP

References:
Configuring SNMP Support > Understanding SNMP > SNMP Versions
Cisco IOS Network Management Command Reference > snmp-server engineID local through snmp trap link-status > snmp-server host

90. Correct Answer: B

Explanation/Reference:
:
It provides neither verification nor encryption. In SNMPv3 there are three combinations of security that can be used: noAuthNoPriv- no verification and no encryption noauth keyword in the configuration
AuthNoPriv - messages are authenticated but not encrypted auth keyword in the configuration
AuthPriv - messages are authenticated and encrypted priv keyword in the configuration
In this case, the keyword noauth in the configuration indicates that no verification and no encryption are provided. This makes the execution no more secure than SNMPv1 or SNMPv2.

In SNMPv1 and SNMPv2, verification is performed using a community string. When you execute SNMP using the noauth keyword, it does not use community strings for verification. Instead it uses the configured user or group name (in this case NORMAL). Regardless, it does not provide either verification or encryption.

Objective:
Infrastructure Services Sub-Objective:
Configure and verify SNMP

References:
SNMP Configuration Guide, Cisco IOS XE Release 3SE (Catalyst 3850 Switches) > SNMPv3

91. Correct Answer: B

Explanation/Reference:
:
While the ip helper address command is typically used to forward DHCP broadcasts to a DHCP server located in a remote subnet, it will also forward the given broadcast packets by default as well:
    TFTP - UDP port 69
    Domain Name System (DNS) UDP port 53 Time service - port 37
    NetBIOS Name Server - port 137 NetBIOS Datagram Server - port 138 Bootstrap Protocol (BOOTP) - port 67 TACACS UDP port 49

Objective:
Infrastructure Services Sub-Objective:
Configure and verify IPv4 and IPv6 DHCP

References:
Cisco IOS IP Application Services Command Reference > ip accounting through ip sctp authenticate > ip helper-address

92. Correct Answer: C

Explanation/Reference:
:
At the end of the command creating the RESTRICTED group is the parameter access 99. This indicates that an access list number 99 is being used to specify the allowed IP addresses of the stations that can be used to connect to the MIB for the group. Since the access list is missing from the configuration, no IP addresses will be allowed, and no connections can be made by the group.

The presence of the keyword priv in the command creating the RESTRICTED group is not causing the issue. This keyword indicates that encryption (privacy) and verification must both be used on all transmissions by the group.

In SMNPv3, there are three combinations of security that can be used:
    noAuthNoPriv- no verification and no encryption noauth keyword in the configuration AuthNoPriv -
    messages are authenticated but not encrypted auth keyword in the configuration AuthPriv -
    messages are authenticated and encrypted priv keyword in the configuration
There is no mismatch among the verification mechanism and the encryption type in the command creating the RESTRICTED user.

snmp-server user RESTRICTED RESTRICTED v3 auth sha CISCO priv des56 CISCO

In the preceding command, the section auth sha CISCO specified that messages are authenticated using SHA with a key of CISCO. It does not need to the match the section priv des56 CISCO, which indicates that encryption (priv) will be provided using DES56 with a key of CISCO.

The presence of the keyword auth in the command creating the RESTRICTED user is not causing the issue. This line indicates that that messages are authenticated using SHA with a key of CISCO.

Objective:

Infrastructure Services Sub-Objective:
Configure and verify SNMP

References:
SNMP Configuration Guide, Cisco IOS XE Release 3SE (Catalyst 3850 Switches) > SNMPv3

93. Correct Answer: A

Explanation/Reference:
:
Translation from IPv6 Internet addresses to an IPv4 network is not supported by the stateless version of NAT64. There are two versions of NAT 64: stateful and stateless. Stateful NAT64 creates or modifies bindings or session state while performing translation, while stateless NAT64 does not create or modify bindings or session state while performing translation/

Translation from IPv4 Internet to an IPv6 network is supported by both NAT64 methods, although the

stateful version requires static 6 to 4 mappings. Translation from an IPv6 network to an IPv4 network is

supported by both methods, stateful and stateless.

Translation from an IPv4 network to an IPv6 network is supported by both methods, although the stateful

version requires static 6-to-4 mappings. Objective:

Infrastructure Services Sub-Objective:
Define IPv6 NAT

References:
Home > Products & services > Cisco IOS and NX-OS software > Cisco IOS Technologies > Enterprise IPv6 solution > Data sheets and literature > NAT64 Technology: Connecting IPv6 and IPv4 Networks

94. Correct Answer: C
Explanation/Reference:
:
The command ip nat inside source list 7 serial0 overload specifies the given:

- The translation must take place in the interface specified as inside.
- It must only be done for inside IP addresses that are specified in access list number 7.
- The IP address that inside addresses must be translated to belongs to the Serial0 interface. The
- translated IP address must be shared by all, as indicated by the overload keyword.

The command ip nat inside identifies the inside interface. In this case, it indicates the one on which translation will take place.

The command ip nat outside identifies the outside interface, which can be configured for translation. However, it has not been configured for translation in this scenario.

The commands below define the inside IP addresses that are allowed to be translated:

```
access-list 7 permit 10.10.10.0 0.0.0.31
access-list 7 permit 10.10.20.0 0.0.0.31
```

Objective:
Infrastructure Services Sub-Objective:
Configure and verify IPv4 Network Address Translation (NAT)

References:
Home > Support >Troubleshooting Technotes > Configuring Network Address Translation: Getting Started Cisco > Cisco IOS IP Application Services Command Reference > ip nat inside source

95. Correct Answer: A

Explanation/Reference:

The command ip nat inside source list 7 serial0 overload specifies the given:

- The translation must take place in the interface specified as inside.
- It must only be done for inside IP addresses that are specified in access list number 7.
- The IP address that inside addresses must be translated to belongs to the Serial0 interface. The translated IP address must be shared by all, as indicated by the overload keyword.

The command ip nat inside identifies the inside interface. In this case, it indicates the one on which translation will take place.

The command ip nat outside identifies the outside interface, which can be configured for translation. However, it has not been configured for translation in this scenario.

The commands below define the inside IP addresses that are allowed to be translated:

```
access-list 7 permit 10.10.10.0 0.0.0.31
access-list 7 permit 10.10.20.0 0.0.0.31
```

Objective:
Infrastructure Services Sub-Objective:
Configure and verify IPv4 Network Address Translation (NAT)

References:
Home > Support >Troubleshooting Technotes > Configuring Network Address Translation: Getting Started Cisco > Cisco IOS IP Application Services Command Reference > ip nat inside source

96. Correct Answer: C

Explanation/Reference:

Network Prefix Translation (NPTv6) is a stateless method of translating the prefix of a received IPv6 address to another prefix without changing the host portion of the IPv6 address. Its mappings are 1 to 1, and it translates only the prefix of the address.

NAT64 translates from IPv6 to IPv4 and vice versa. It does not translate from IPv6 to IPv6.

NAT44 translates from IPv4 to IPv4. It does not translate from IPv6 to IPv6.

There is IPv4 version of Network Prefix Translation, called NPTv4. IT does not translate from IPv6 to

IPv6. Objective:
Infrastructure Services Sub-Objective:
Define IPv6 NAT

References:
RFC 6296 > IPv6-to-IPv6 Network Prefix Translation
Cisco > Publications and Merchandise > The Internet Protocol Journal > Issues > Volume 14, Number 2, June 2011 > IPv6 Site Multihoming

97. Correct Answer: C

Explanation/Reference:
:
One is the number of the HSRP group. Hot Standby Routing Protocol (HSRP) can be used to provide default gateway redundancy for computers sharing the same gateway. At least two routers are gathered into a routing group, which in this case is numbered 1. One of the routers will answer ARP requests for the standby IP address (in this case 171.16.6.100), which is the address the computers will have configured as their default gateway. That router is called the active router. If that router goes down, then the other router will start answering ARP requests for the standby IP address.

This is not a Gateway Load Balancing Protocol configuration. That is an alternative to HSRP which allows both routers to be used while still providing backup to one another. That configuration could be different in that it uses GLBP groups rather than standby groups, amongst other differences.

This router will be not prevented from taking back over as active router when it recovers from an outage of its Serial 0 interface. The presence of the command standby 1 preempt indicates that the router can take back over or preempt the other router when it recovers from an outage of its Serial 0 interface. The command standby 1 track Serial0 tells the router to track the up/down state of its Serial 0 interface. If it goes down, it knows to decrement its HSRP priority by 10 (the decrement value). This will drop its HSRP priority to 95. We do not see the priority of the other router in the group, but if for example its priority is 100, this configuration could allow it to take over as active router.

Objective:
Infrastructure Services Sub-Objective:
Configure and verify tracking objects

References:
Home > Support > Technology support > IP > IP application services > Troubleshoot and alerts > Troubleshooting Technotes > How to Use the standby preempt and standby track Commands

98. Correct Answer: C

Explanation/Reference:
:
The router will send NTP broadcast on its E0/0 interface. The command ntp broadcast, when performed under an interface, instructs the router to send NTP broadcast packets on the interface. Any devices on the network that are set with the ntp broadcast client command on any interface will be listening for these NTP broadcasts. While the clients will not respond in any way, they will use the information in the NTP broadcast packets to synchronize their clocks with the information.

The time zone is not set to 8 hours less than Pacific Standard Time. The value -8 in the command clock timezone PST -8 is the amount of hours offset from UTC time, not from the time zone stated in the command.

The router will not listen for NTP broadcasts on the interface E0/0. The ntp broadcast command, when performed under an interface, instructs the router to send NTP broadcast packets on the interface. To set the interface to listen and use NTP broadcasts, you could execute the ntp broadcast client command on the interface.

The router will not periodically update its software clock. The command ntp update-calendar configures the system to update its hardware clock from the software clock at periodic intervals.

Objective:
Infrastructure Services Sub-Objective:
Configure and verify Network Time Protocol (NTP)

References:
Basic System Management > Setting Time and Calendar Services > Configuring NTP

99. Correct Answer: B

Explanation/Reference:
:
The partial output of the show run command indicates that the port number of the HTTPS interface has been changed to 1025. This is indicted by the presence of this command in the configuration:

```
ip http secure-port 1025
```

That is not the default port configuration of 443. Therefore, anyone wishing to connect to the secure server will need to reference the new port number in the command. If you change the HTTPS port number, clients attempting to connect to the HTTPS server needs to specify the port number in the URL, in this format:

https://device:port_number

In this syntax, port_number is the HTTPS port number.

It will not help for the technician to reference port 443 in the command, because that is no longer the port

number of the secure server. It is now 1025. It is not crucial to disable the HTTP server to use the HTTPS

server, although it is a best practice to do so.

There is no need to enable the secure server. We can see it has been enabled by the presence of this command in the configuration:

```
ip http secure-server
```

Objective:
Infrastructure Services Sub-Objective:
Configure and verify device management

References:
Cisco IOS HTTP Services Command Reference > clear ip http client cookie through show ip http server secure status > ip http secure-port

100. Correct Answer: AC

Explanation/Reference:
:
The two commands that needs to have been performed to produce output in that format are logging console level notifications and service timestamps log datetime msec.

The logging console level notifications command species that all messages at level 5 (notifications and above) will be sent to the console. This is not entered by the number of the message type, but the name of the message type.

The service timestamps log datetime msec command specifies that a timestamp up to the millisecond

must be included in all messages that include the time. While the logging console level command can be

used with a level number on some devices, notifications are level 5, not 4.

The service timestamps log datetime command specifies that a timestamp must be included in all messages, but it will not include the millisecond. Better logging functionality can be achieved by using the msec keyword to help organize tightly spaced events.

The logging history command can specify the proper level of messages to reduce unnecessary

messages. Objective:

Infrastructure Services Sub-Objective:
Configure and verify logging

References:
Catalyst 2960 and 2960-S Software Configuration Guide, 12.2(55)SE > Configuring System Message Logging Cisco > Cisco IOS Embedded Syslog Manager Command Reference > logging console
Cisco > Cisco IOS Configuration Fundamentals Command Reference > R through setup > service timestamps

101. Correct Answer: B

Explanation/Reference:
:
Network Prefix Translation (NPTv6) is a stateless method of translating the prefix of a received IPv6 address to another prefix without changing the host portion of the IPv6 address. Some of its features are:
- It supports both transports that perform checksums on the IP header and those that do not. It provides
- a 1 to 1 relationship among the inside and outside prefixes.
- It translates only the prefix, and not the entire address.

Objective:
Infrastructure Services Sub-Objective:
Define IPv6 NAT

References:
Cisco > Publications and Merchandise > The Internet Protocol Journal > Issues > Volume 14, Number 2, June 2011 > IPv6 Site Multihoming Howfunky...a place with useless technical content!>IPv6 to IPv6 Network Prefix Translation or NPTv6

102. Correct Answer: C

Explanation/Reference:
:
NAT64 is a solution when IPv6 hosts need to communicate with IPv4-only servers. When the translation take place on the router the IPv4 address 10.0.0.1 will converted to hex as a00:1 and will be attached to the end of the stateful prefix of 3001::/96 that was configured on the router interface connected to the IPv4 server. The result will be 3001::a00:1.

The address will not be 2001::a001. The prefix that will be attached to the hex version of 10.0.0.1 will not be that of the interface fa0/2/7 but will be the prefix that was configured on that interface for nat64 translation which is 3301::/96.

The address will not be 2001::a00:b. That is the IPv6 address on the interface connected to the IPv6 host, but that address is not used for IPv4 to IPv6 communication. A translated address will be generated by converting the IPv4 address of the IPv4 host to hex and attaching it to the IPv6 prefix configured on the interface connected to the IPv4 server.

The address will not be 2001::A00:A. That is the IPv6 address of the IPv6 host. That was statically mapped to 10.0.0.10 in the configuration and as such will be the IPv4 address used by the IPv6 host on the IPv4 side of the router.

Objective:

Infrastructure Services Sub-Objective:
Define IPv6 NAT

References:
Stateful Network Address Translation 64 (PDF)

103. Correct Answer: D

Explanation/Reference:

One of the features of stateful NAT64 is that it conserves IPv4 addresses. NAT64 is a version of network address translation that translates IPv6 address to IPv4 and vice versa. It has two variants, stateless and stateful. The given table defines some of the major differences among the two:

Stateless NAT64	Stateful NAT64
1:1 translation, hence applicable for limited number of endpoints	1: N translation, hence no constraint on the number of end points
No conservation of IPv4 address	Conserves IPv4 address
Helps ensure end-to-end address transparency and scalability	Uses address overloading; hence lacks end-to-end address transparency
No state or bindings created on the translation	State or bindings created on every unique translation

NAT64 has neither the variant static nor the variant manual.

Objective:
Infrastructure Services Sub-Objective:
Define IPv6 NAT

References:
Home > Products & services > Cisco IOS and NX-OS software > Cisco IOS technologies > Enterprise ipv6 solution > Data sheets and literature > White papers > NAT64 Technology: Connecting IPv6 and IPv4 Networks > Technologies Facilitating IPv6/IPv4 Translation

104. Correct Answer: C

Explanation/Reference:

Stateless NAT64 does not support translating from the IPv6 Internet to an IPv4 network. NAT64 is a version of network address translation that translates IPv6 address to IPv4 and vice versa. It has two variants, stateless and stateful. In stateless translation, mappings are created using an algorithm, but those mappings are not maintained while translation is being performed. Stateful NAT64 both creates and maintains mappings during translation.

Due to the fact it does not maintain mappings, stateless NAT64 supports all of the options given except

translating from the IPv6 Internet to an IPv4 network. Objective:
Infrastructure Services Sub-Objective:
Define IPv6 NAT

References:
Home > Products & services > Cisco IOS and NX-OS software > Cisco IOS technologies > Enterprise ipv6 solution > Data sheets and literature > White papers >

NAT64 Technology: Connecting IPv6 and IPv4 Networks > Technologies Facilitating IPv6/IPv4 Translation

105. Correct Answer: A

Explanation/Reference:
:
The ICMP path echo operation discovers the path using the traceroute command, and then measures response time among the source router and each intermittent hop in the path. IP SLAs allow users to monitor network performance among Cisco routers or from either a Cisco router to a remote IP device.

The Internet Control Message Protocol (ICMP) Echo Operation measures end-to-end response time among a Cisco router and any IP-enabled device. Response time is computed by measuring the time taken among sending an ICMP echo request message to the destination and receiving an ICMP echo reply. It does not measure hop-by-hop response time.

The UDP Jitter Operation for VoIP is an extension to the current jitter operations with specific enhancements for VoIP. The enhancements allow this operation to calculate voice quality scores and simulate the codec's directly in CLI and the MIB. It does not measure hop-by-hop response time.

The UDP Jitter Operation is designed to measure the delay, delay variance, and packet loss in IP networks by generating active UDP traffic. It does not measure hop-by-hop response time.

Objective:
Infrastructure Services Sub-Objective:
Define SLA architecture

References:
Home > Support > Technology support > IP > IP application services > Technology information > Technology white paper > Cisco IOS IP Service Level Agreements User Guide

106. Correct Answer: A

Explanation/Reference:
:
It will find the response time to resolve the DNS name cow.cisco.com. Domain Name System (DNS) response time is computed by calculating the difference among the time taken to send a DNS request and the time a reply is received. The Cisco IOS IP SLAs DNS operation queries for an IP address if the user specifies a hostname, or queries for a hostname if the user specifies an IP address.

It will not find the response time to connect to the DNS server at 10.52.128.30. That is the IP address of the DNS server being used for the operation (10.52.128.30). However, it will measure the response time to resolve the DNS name cow.cisco.com.

It will not start in one minute. It will start immediately, as indicated by the start-time now parameter.

It will not gather data for one minute. The numeral 1 in the first line refers to the IP SLA number, and the numeral 1 in the last line refers to the IP SLA number to be scheduled.

Objective:
Infrastructure Services Sub-Objective:
Configure and verify IP SLA

References:
Home > Support > Technology support > IP > IP application services > Technology information > Technology white paper > Cisco IOS IP Service Level Agreements User Guide

107. Correct Answer: C

Explanation/Reference:
:
Sixty-one packets were dropped because the send queue was full. The last line in the output, 61 export packets were dropped due to output drops, will result when the send queue is full.

Fifteen packets were not dropped because there was insufficient memory to create the export packet. Drops that take placered from insufficient memory are indicated with the line 3 flows failed due to lack of export packet, and there were only three of them.

Three export packets were not dropped because CEF was unable to switch or forward the packet to the process level. Drops that take placered because CEF was unable to switch or forward the packet, are indicated with the line 15 export packets were dropped due to no fib, and there were fifteen of them.

Eleven flows were sent, not eight. The eleven flows were sent in eight datagrams.

Objective:
Infrastructure Services Sub-Objective:
Configure and verify Cisco NetFlow

References:
Cisco > Cisco IOS NetFlow Command Reference > show ip flow export
Home > Products & services > Cisco IOS and NX-OS software > Cisco IOS Technologies > Management instrumentation > Cisco IOS NetFlow > Data sheets and literature > Introduction to Cisco IOS NetFlow - A Technical Overview

108. Correct Answer: A

Explanation/Reference:
:
The given command sequence is correct:

Router1(config)# service dhcp Router1(config)# ip dhcp pool IPPool
Router1(dhcp-config)# network 10.10.0.0 255.255.0.0 Router1(dhcp-config)# domain-name Cisco
Router1(dhcp-config)# dns-server 10.10.0.1
Router1(dhcp-config)# default-router 10.10.0.1 Router1(dhcp-config)# exit
Router1(config)# ip dhcp excluded-address 10.10.0.20 10.10.0.25

The Router1(config)# service dhcp command enables the DHCP process. It is enabled by default, but this

command may be needed if it has been disabled. The Router1(config)# ip dhcp pool IPPool command

creates a DHCP pool named IPPool.

The Router1(dhcp-config)# network 10.10.0.0 255.255.0.0 command specifies the subnet and mask for which the DHCP process will be handing out IP addresses. Unless otherwise specified, it is assumed that the assignment will start with the first address on the subnet and end with the last address on the subnet; in this case,
10.10.0.1 through 10.10.0.255.

The Router1(dhcp-config)# domain-name Cisco command sets the domain name for the clients to "Cisco."

The Router1(dhcp-config)# dns-server 10.10.0.1 command sets the DNS server IP address for the clients

to 10.10.0.1. The Router1(dhcp-config)# default-router 10.10.0.1 command sets the default gateway for

the clients to 10.10.0.1.

The Router1(dhcp-config)# exit command exits back to worldwide config mode.

The Router1(config)# ip dhcp excluded-address 10.10.0.20 10.10.0.25 command configures the DHCP process not to hand out addresses 10.10.0.20 through
10.10.0.25 so that there is no conflict with the print servers. This command is technically not a dhcp-config command, but if it is issued in the dhcp-config mode, the router will exit to worldwide config mode and

invoke the command.

The other options are incorrect due to incorrect syntax or command mode. Objective:
Infrastructure Services Sub-Objective:
Configure and verify IPv4 and IPv6 DHCP

References:
Cisco > Cisco IOS IP Addressing Services Configuration Guide, Release 12.4 > Part 3: DHCP > DHCP Overview

109. Correct Answer: A

Explanation/Reference:
:
DNS64 and NAT64 functions are completely separated when using NAT64. In NAT-PT these two functions are tightly coupled, which reduces flexibility and is why NAT-PT has been deprecated, with the IETF proposing NAT64 as its viable successor.

DNS64 and NAT64 functions are not completely integrated in NAT64, so this is not an advantage of NAT64 over NAT-PT as a translation option.

NAT64 works over non- Ethernet networks. It is NAT-PT that does only works on Ethernet networks.

Therefore, this is not an advantage of NAT 64 over NAT-PT. NAT64 can reconstruct fragments packets

if they are fragmented by an intermediate IPv4 router. It is NAT-PT that will be unable to reconstruct

fragments packets if

they are fragmented by an intermediate IPv4 router, so this is not an advantage of NAT 64 over NAT-PT.

Objective:
Infrastructure Services Sub-Objective:
Define IPv6 NAT

References:
Home > Products & services > Cisco IOS and NX-OS software > Cisco IOS technologies > Enterprise IPv6 solution > Data sheets and literature > White papers > NAT64 Technology: Connecting IPv6 and IPv4 Networks > Technologies Facilitating IPv6/IPv4 Translation

110. Correct Answer: C

Explanation/Reference:
:
The IP SLA TCP connect operation is used to gather statistics on connection-oriented services. The tcp-connect 10.0.0.1 23 control disable command specifies the IP address to which the responder must respond, the port number on which to respond and it disables the control protocol normally used to inform the responder to temporarily enable the port specified .by the configuration in the sender. When the responder is a non-Cisco device, a well-known port number needs to be chosen and the control protocol must be disabled on the responder. When a Cisco device is the responder, then any port number can be chosen and the control protocol must be left enabled.

The frequency 30 command specifies how often the test must take place in seconds. It is not changed in any way as a result of the responder being a non-Cisco device.

The timeout 1000 command specifies in milliseconds the amount of time an IP SLAs operation waits for a response from its request packet. It is not changed in any way as a result of the responder being a non-Cisco device.

The tag FLL-RO command simply applies a user-specified identifier to the IP SLAs operation and is changed in any way as a result of the responder being a non- Cisco device.

Objective:
Infrastructure Services Sub-Objective:
Configure and verify IP SLA

References:
IP SLAs Configuration Guide, Cisco IOS Release 15M&T > Configuring IP SLAs TCP Connect Operations
Cisco > Cisco IOS IP SLAs Command Reference > tcp-connect

111. Correct Answer: C
Explanation/Reference:
:
The ip sla reset command is not mandatory for an execution plan to configure IP SLAs for monitoring IP connections and traffic. This command causes the IP SLA engine to either restart or shutdown. As a result, all IP SLAs operations are stopped, IP SLA configuration information is erased, and IP SLAs are restarted.
The IP SLAs configuration information will need to be reloaded to the engine. The given commands are

crucial to the execution plan:

ip sla
ip sla schedule

icmp-echo

The ip sla command allows you to configure IP SLAs operations. When you execute this command in the worldwide configuration mode, it enables the IP SLA configuration mode. In the IP SLA configuration mode, you can configure different IP SLA operations. You can configure up to 2000 operations for a given IP SLA ID number.

The icmp-echo command allows you to monitor IP connections and traffic on routers by creating an IP SLA ICMP Echo operation. This operation monitors end-to- end response times among routers.

The ip sla schedule command allows you to schedule the IP SLA operation that has been configured. With this command, you can specify when the operation starts, how long the operation runs, and the how long the operation gathers information. For example, if you execute the ip sla schedule 40 start-time now life forever command, the IP SLA operation with the identification number 40 immediately starts running. This is because the now keyword is specified for the start-time parameter. The forever keyword with the life parameter indicates that the operation keeps collecting information indefinitely. Note that you cannot re-configure the IP SLA operation after you have performed the ip sla schedule command.

The information gathered by an IP SLA operation is typically stored in RTTMON-MIB. A Management Information Base (MIB) is a database hosting information crucial for the management of routers or network devices. The RTTMON-MIB is a Cisco-defined MIB intended for Cisco IOS IP SLAs. RTTMON MIB acts as an interface among the Network Management System (NMS) applications and the Cisco IOS IP SLAs operations.

Objective:
Infrastructure Services Sub-Objective:
Configure and verify IP SLA

References:
Cisco > Support > Technology Support > IP > IP Application Services > Technology Information > Technology White Paper > Cisco IOS IP Service Level Agreements User Guide
Cisco IOS IP SLAs Command Reference > icmp-echo through probe-packet priority > ip sla

112. Correct Answer: A
Explanation/Reference:
:
By tracking the loopback interface and decrementing the priority if it goes down, technicians could have a method of moving the active role to the other router by disabling the loopback interface. This method is less disruptive than disabling any of the physical interfaces. Although no decrement value has been specified, a default decrement of 10 will take place.

This configuration could not be used to prevent this router from ever relinquishing the active role. That could defeat the purpose of Hot Standby Routing Protocol (HSRP), which is to provide failover by relinquishing the active role to the other router.

This configuration could not be used to prevent this router from ever performing the active role. That could defeat the purpose of HSRP which is to provide failover by this router taking the active role when there is an issue with the other router.

This configuration could not be used to allow preemption over multiple peers. When more than two routers are in an HSRP group, the active router is allowed preemption over multiple peers by default.

Objective:
Infrastructure Services Sub-Objective:
Configure and verify tracking objects

References:
Home > Support > Technology support > IP > IP application services > Troubleshoot and alerts > Troubleshooting Technotes > How to use the standby preempt and standby track commands

113. Correct Answer: A
Explanation/Reference:
:
Any IP SLA operations accuracy can be enhanced by configure an IP SLA responder on the destination device. It is important to note that only Cisco devices support the configuration as a responder.

You do not configure an IP SLA responder on the source device. You schedule the operation on the source device and the destination device is the one that is configured as a responder.

You do not schedule the operation on the destination device. You schedule the operation on the source device and the destination device is the one that is configured as a responder.

Adding the verify-data command to the configuration of the operation will not enhance the accuracy of the information gathered. When data verification is enabled, each operation response is checked for corruption. Use the verify-data command with caution during normal operations because it generates unnecessary overhead.

Objective: Infrastructure Services

Sub-Objective:
Configure and verify IP SLA

References:
IP SLAs Configuration Guide, Cisco IOS Release 15M > Configuring IP SLAs TCP Connect Operations

References:
Configuring SNMP Support > Understanding SNMP > SNMP Versions
Cisco IOS Network Management Command Reference > snmp-server engineID local through snmp trap link-status > snmp-server host

Lightning Source UK Ltd.
Milton Keynes UK
UKHW051941240622
404939UK00003B/108